Lay Low and Don't Make the Big Mistake

The Lazy Person's Guide to Success on the Job

**BRIAN HARRIS AND
RICH HERSCHLAG**

Illustrations by Travis Foster

A FIRESIDE BOOK/*Published by Simon & Schuster*

ACKNOWLEDGMENTS

Thanks, Martin and Diana Harris, for doing Brian's seventh-grade algebra homework. Thanks, Jack and Judy Herschlag, for filling out Rich's college applications. Thanks, Sue Herschlag, for retyping the manuscript while Rich slept in the TV room. Thanks, James and Dolores Ladop and Susan Pearce for prying Brian off of the couch and placing him in front of the computer. Thank you, John Ware, for doing all the legwork. Thank you, Sarah Baker, for turning a string of offhand observations into a book. Thanks, Lisa Meyers, for letting us crash. And thank you to the many nameless people who contributed the bulk of the ideas in this book. According to our lawyer, you'll have to *remain* nameless.

Fireside
Rockefeller Center
1230 Avenue of the Americas
New York, NY 10020

FIRESIDE and colophon are registered trademarks of Simon & Schuster Inc.

Designed by Paula R. Szafranski

Manufactured in the United States of America

1   3   5   7   9   10   8   6   4   2

Library of Congress Cataloging-in-Publication Data
Harris, Brian, date
Lay low and don't make the big mistake : the lazy person's guide
to success on the job / Brian Harris and Rich Herschlag.
p.   cm.
1. Success in business—United States—Humor.   I. Herschlag,
Rich, 1962–   . II. Title.
HF5386.H2725   1997
650.14′02′07—dc21   97-3206
CIP
ISBN 0-684-83491-X

Contents

Getting Away . . . With All Sorts of Stuff

Getting Out: And Now the End Is Near . . .

GETTING WITH THE PROGRAM
An Introduction

A Lazy History

Learning from the Past

Starting with our Puritan forefathers, Americans have long valued the virtues of industriousness and hard work. But America was not built solely on the backs of the hardworking. The propped-up feet of lazy people have been responsible for much of the advancement in our workplace and society. After all, it was a lazy man (or woman) who first sat back and thought: "There's got to be an easier way."

Back in the days when there was only one type of job opening—"hunter-gatherer"—success was achieved by those tribes who traveled the farthest in search of ever more elusive harvest and hunting grounds. Then one day some indolent prehistoric chieftain thought, "Hey, wait a second. All this hunting and gathering is tiring me out. How 'bout next time we capture a few animals and ride them home before we eat them? And when we get home, let's see what happens if we put some of those seeds in little rows in the ground." Thus, transportation and agriculture, two pillars of civilization, were born.

A Debt of Gratitude

Since that time, stunning achievements have sprung from lazy minds, yielding more progress than hardworking folks might like to admit. Take the modern printing press, invented by the irrepressibly lazy Johannes Gutenberg. Before his groundbreaking invention in the fifteenth century, books had to be meticulously transcribed by hand, page after tedious page. "Scribe" was one of the most valued occupations of the time, for without these industrious folks, important information had to be disseminated by word of mouth. It was Gutenberg who said, "This scribing is making my hand hurt. Can't we get a machine to do this instead?"

Three hundred years later and a couple of hundred miles to the north, Sir Isaac Newton discovered gravity while snoozing under an apple tree. Later he was having a hard time going through all the math to prove his theories, so he invented calculus as a shortcut. A century after that, across the Atlantic, Eli Whitney was getting bored pulling seeds out of cotton by hand and thought up a clever little device which allowed the cotton industry to become the backbone of the Southern economy. And around the beginning of this century, tiring of filling his oil lamp, Thomas Alva Edison invented the light bulb. Meanwhile, Henry Ford, realizing it took too long to make one car at a time, designed the modern factory method.

> **I**t was Gutenberg who said, "This scribing is making my hand hurt."

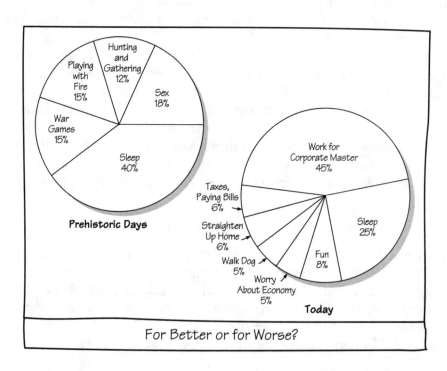

For Better or for Worse?

Reversal of Fortune

Yet despite these historical contributions, alarming trends have been in evidence more recently in the American workplace that are threatening the survival of the truly lazy. In 1970, the average American workweek was thirty-seven hours. Twenty-seven years later, the American workweek now stands at fifty-two hours, an increase of 40 percent. What has all this extra work gained us? Is it merely a coincidence that in the years since the 1960s, U.S. productivity has grown at its lowest rate in history? Why have we turned our backs on the lazy person and his unique contribution to society?

In a way we've come full circle. What is the purpose of all this progress but to free us from the usual grind of eking out an existence? Yet each day represents a siege—once you finish with work, the daily commute, and a bit of grocery shopping or laundry, there's not even time left for a normal ten hours of sleep.

A successful hunter-gatherer society, in contrast, works an average of thirty hours a week, the rest of the time spent chatting with friends, sleeping and general luxuriating. For all our "progress," we're really no better off than we were ten thousand years ago. Lazy people in particular are significantly worse off. So keep reading. Or consider relocating to the heart of the Amazon.

The Lazy Person:
The Last Best Hope

Thicker than Water

In a world gone mad, where brutal workweeks are the norm and where people, political parties, and nations are in perpetual conflict, our greatest hope may lie in the lazy. The lazy number in the tens, even hundreds, of millions, and represent the broadest possible cross-section of people that our country—or planet—has ever known. The lazy can be found in every ethnic, racial, or religious groups; both genders; and every social, economic, and political division. Lazy people of all ages and walks of life share a common interest greater and stronger than the forces of language or culture: the drive to get from point A to point B with minimal effort . . . or even to consider simply remaining at point A.

> The lazy can be found in every ethnic, racial, or religious group.

It is this connection that will inspire someone to transcend the boundaries of skin color or headdress and yell: "Hey, hold the elevator!" It is this link that will allow an individual to rise above mutual suspicion and say: "Wake me if someone comes." It is precisely this commonality, this universal tie that will enable us all to lift our hands, pick up the phone, dial our co-worker, and say: "Tell the boss I won't be coming in today."

Look, Up in the Sky

While not exactly a comic book superhero, the lazy person enjoys a good comic book, especially at work. Yes, the lazy person—he's back, and he doesn't like what he sees. So he's declared a revolution. Not a violent, noisy one in the halls of Congress, but a quiet, unassuming one where it counts: in the workplace—*your* workplace. To facilitate this revolution, he and, yes, *she*, have hired a couple of ghostwriters to write a book—*this* book.

Lay Low and Don't Make the Big Mistake diagnoses the disease and prescribes the cure. From "Faking the Commute" to "The Art of Calling In Sick" to "Camouflaging the Lazy Person's Office" to "Your Boss's Vacation = Your Vacation," *Lay Low* pulls no punches in making life enjoyable again for Americans of all professions. Although these ideas may appear new, they have been forming in our collective unconscious for quite some time. It is the pooling of this valuable knowledge that makes *Lay Low* perhaps our greatest weapon in the all-important fight to reclaim our lives, our relationships, and our midday naps.

Lay Low: Correct and Incorrect

Who Are the Lazy?

Fifteen Traits of the Truly *Lazy*

Many people consider themselves to be lazy, but in fact display only a few indolent tendencies, not an overriding character trait. To test your own laziness, try the following quiz:

QUESTION	YES	NO
Do you consider having a steady job to be a sign of personal failure?	❑	❑
Do you consistently maintain LIFO (Last In–First Out) work hours?	❑	❑
Do you consider reading the newspaper to be a crucial part of your job responsibilities?	❑	❑
Do you consider the remote control second only to the electric foot massager as the greatest invention in Western civilization?	❑	❑
Do you refuse to own any pet requiring higher maintenance than a rock?	❑	❑
Do you refuse the joy of parenthood, unless the child is old enough to support you?	❑	❑
Does the cold cut sandwich reside on the frontier of your culinary abilities?	❑	❑
Do you have *PGA Golf, Flight Simulator,* or *Civilization* on your computer at work?	❑	❑
Do you live in an apartment complex or condominium, refusing to submit to the bonds of home ownership?	❑	❑

QUESTION	YES	NO
Do you maintain a minimum of nine hours' sleep per night? Ten on weekends? Three during work hours?	❏	❏
Is buying new underwear vs. washing the old ones a tough call?	❏	❏
Do you drive to get to where you jog?	❏	❏
Do you wonder how people got along before the invention of paper plates?	❏	❏
Do you consider hiding under your pillow when woken up by a smoke alarm?	❏	❏
Does your breakfast of champions consist of last week's coffee and last night's pizza crust?	❏	❏

TOTAL [   ]

SCORING

"YES" TOTAL

0–2: **Workaholic.** Why are you reading this book? You have more productive things to do with your time. Or at least you *think* you do! Get a life.

3–7: **Industrious.** You might have the vestiges of a life, but you wouldn't mind coming into work on weekends to straighten up the office and prepare for the next week.

8–11: **Sort of Lazy.** You could probably benefit from this book. Still, you're not immune to taking on additional "responsibility."

12–15: **Truly Lazy!** You are that rare gem in the workforce. Now if you can only discipline yourself to continue reading this book rather than going to the remote control.

Famous Successful
Lazy People

Calvin Coolidge

Our idol. America's thirtieth president was renowned for sleeping an average of fourteen hours per day. One of President Coolidge's favorite sayings was, "If you see twelve problems coming down the road, rest assured that eleven of them will fall by the side before reaching you." So much for "proactive" thinking. Coolidge was so lazy that when he died four years after leaving office, Gertrude Stein remarked, "Coolidge dead? How can you tell?"

Regardless, the country performed exceedingly well during the six years that Coolidge was president. Coolidge's presidency—the Roaring Twenties, flappers, high economic growth, low inflation, sexual morality that would make the sixties seem stuffy—was frankly a lot of fun. The country was doing fine and President Coolidge didn't want to mess things up. In typical laconic Coolidge fashion, he decided not to seek reelection, simply stating, "I choose not to run." And good thing, too. Look what happened to his hardworking successor—Herbert Hoover.

Babe Ruth

Take a look at any photo of him after about 1927. 'Nuff said.

Ronald Reagan

Another prodigious sleeper, our fortieth president shares much in common with our thirtieth. In fact, one of Reagan's first acts as president was to hang a prominent portrait of Calvin Coolidge in the White House. Reagan reveled in his laziness—remarking about how he would on a particularly tough day have to "burn the midday oil." Although Reagan didn't quite measure up to Coolidge in maintaining a solid fourteen hours of sleep day in and day out, Reagan did almost sleep though his inauguration.

John Lennon

Almost all rock musicians are lazy, but only John Lennon came up with the idea of a "sleep in" to protest the Vietnam War.

Abraham Lincoln

Abraham Lincoln, the self-made man who worked his way up from a log cabin to the White House, lazy? Yes. While president, Lincoln often would not be seen for days on end, as he would cloister himself in the private quarters of the White House and not communicate with anybody. Rumor had it that the president would be loafing around and sleeping through these periods. Then there's the Gettysburg Address. Did Lincoln slave over the speech, refining it for days on end like a modern-day president would? No, he just scratched it onto the back of an envelope and read it a few hours later.

Jack Kerouac

This famous writer and inadvertent leader of the Beat Generation spent most of his time drinking, riding around in borrowed cars, and making "insight" into other people doing the same. The "Beat" refers to the cool jazz he and his pals grooved to, not to how he felt at the end of a hard day at the office. You see, Old Jack never held down a job for more than a couple of months.

Andy Warhol

Andy believed that anything, including fame, could be achieved and discarded in fifteen minutes. Thanks to him, a big picture of a can of soup now passes for art.

John Cage

Though a highly successful composer, Cage was too lazy to be bothered with complicated musical scores and hard-to-master instruments like the violin and cello. Instead, he threw together a bunch of tin cans and an old piano to "see what would happen."

George Foreman

Eats lots of hamburgers and fights thirty-six minutes a year . . . if it lasts that long.

Boris Yeltsin

Having the economy run by the free market and the Russian mob means a lot less work for Boris, and he likes it that way. This leaves lots of opportunities for monthlong benders, which the Russian press politely calls "disappearances."

Typical Work Conditions
Through the Ages

Prehistoric Hunter-Gatherer Societies

There wasn't yet a well-articulated language, so no one could tell you to gather data, perform a linear regression, and have a report on his desk by three. Overall, life was pretty "civilized" as long as conditions were suitable for hunting and gathering. If so, you could finish up the day's work in a few hours, leaving the rest of the day for putting graffiti on cave walls, having sex, and dozing off. The trick was picking the right location. Hunting and gathering in the tundra, for example, was probably not much fun.

Ancient Egypt

Good if you were the Pharaoh. Otherwise not so good. Ever try building a pyramid without power tools?

Ancient Jews

Bad while wandering in the desert. Worse while in captivity (see above). Being the "Chosen People" wasn't always so easy.

Ancient Greece

Not bad, especially in Athens, whose citizens had plenty of free time on their hands for studying triangles, the diameter of a circle, and each other. They put on lots of plays about birds and frogs and things, preferring lounging around

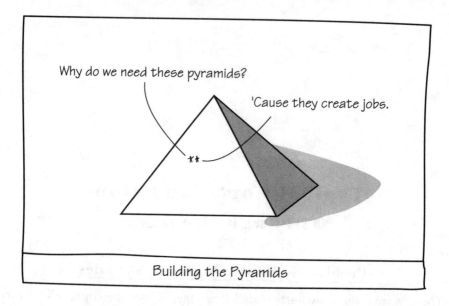

Why do we need these pyramids?

'Cause they create jobs.

Building the Pyramids

in an amphitheater to the rigors of hard work. The Greeks' leisurely philosophy was best embodied by Socrates, who asked lots of questions, but let other people worry about the answers.

Ancient Rome

Good if you were a Roman, not so good if you were from somewhere else in the empire where you had to work to support Rome's decadence. Best if you were a member of the Roman nobility, who seemed to raise decadence to an art form: orgies, vomitoriums, gladiator fights, etc.

Medieval Europe

Fairly arduous, with lots of building and defending castles going on. "Feudal" and "futile" went pretty much hand in hand. Things got even worse when the bubonic plague hit, with the constant collection and burial of corpses becoming practically a second job.

The Vikings

Unpleasant with all that rowing back and forth across the North Sea, with time off only for looting and pillaging.

The Aztecs

A mixed bag. Like the ancient Egyptians, the Aztecs employed slave labor to construct their enormous public monuments. But those slaves had to be *captured* first, and then ultimately replaced after they were sacrificed. Thus, an Aztec's work was never done.

Sixteenth-Century Spain

Spain looted the Aztecs and had huge gold reserves, allowing Spaniards to kick back for a hundred years until the booty ran out.

Colonial America

No fun at all. Work all year for one turkey dinner, while stern-faced Puritans scowled at you and printed scarlet letters on your face.

Plains Indians

Not bad. The buffalo provided for all their needs: food, clothing, building materials, and area rugs. The Plains Indians took one-stop shopping to new heights.

Victorian England

According to Oliver Twist, not so good. Birthplace of the term "sweatshop."

Nineteenth-Century China

Although heavily influenced by industrious Victorian England, there was a bright side. An entire *tenth* of the adult population was holed up in opium dens, doing no work whatsoever.

The Soviet Union

The most popular joke of the former Soviet Union was, "The State pretends to pay us, so we pretend to work."

GETTING STARTED
Hit the Ground Walking

The No-Sweat Job Search

Reality Bites . . .

Sadly, even lazy people must find a way to put food on the table. For the vast majority who aren't members of the landed aristocracy, this means actually finding a job. This task is made doubly difficult for the lazy person. Unlike the typical person, who is only interested in finding a job, the lazy person must find an easy job easily.

. . . So Bite Back

Although it's hard to avoid a bit of "glistening" (as Orson Welles once said, "Miss Hayworth does not sweat; she glistens") in creating a résumé, your initial or "front-loaded" efforts will pay off with less work later on. (See "The Lazy Person's Guide to Résumés.") The next step is to put together a list of potential employers. Help-wanted ads are a good idea, as is the bulletin board in the Laundromat. Ideally, you can step into a position being vacated by a friend or relative, saving everybody a lot of trouble.

> **I**deally, you can step into a position being vacated by a friend or relative, saving everybody a lot of trouble.

You'll need a good cover letter, but of course you don't want to waste a lot of time writing one. Instead, get someone to do it for you. Put an ad in the newspaper for the type of job you are looking for. You'll be amazed at the brilliant and articulate letters that pour in. Pick out the best one and go with it. Or, if you're too lazy even to put in a fake ad, we've provided a time-tested sample letter. Just fill in the blanks and you're off to a great start.

Dear (*contact person*):

I read your ad in the (*name of publication*) with great interest. I have (*number from dartboard*) years experience as a (*whatever they're looking for*) and believe I would be an asset to your firm. I feel that I have maximized my potential in my (*number from dartboard, lower than first number*) years at (*name of fictitious, untraceable firm*) and as a result am seeking a greater challenge at (*name of firm you're applying to*).

I have a degree in (*relevant subject your parents told you to major in*) and am a certified (*whatever they want you to be certified in*). During my career, I have focused on (*something boring and pertinent*) and look forward to continuing on that track. To date, my most notable achievement has been (*something more impressive than selecting a long-distance phone carrier*). Like (*name of firm you're applying to*), I am project oriented and place a premium on maximizing timeliness and efficiency.

I can best be reached by phone on (*days and times you're not playing miniature golf*). I look forward to hearing from you.

Yours truly,
(*your name*)

In today's economy, the important thing when submitting a cover letter is that you remember a single overriding fact: The firm offering the job—no matter how menial or demanding that job may be—has the pick of the litter. If you're a board-certified neurosurgeon with eight rather than the required ten years of experience in ophthalmic ganglion-reattachment surgery, you can look forward to a polite form letter and another year of hanging out at the mall. So if you can't actually be what they want, at least sound like what they want.

If you can't actually be what they want, at least sound like what they want.

If you're particularly adventurous, particularly fed up with the system, and particularly lazy, you might want to skip the whole cover letter effort. Call the company directly. Tell them you're returning their call to set up an interview. They will likely be too embarrassed to admit even the possibility that they lost your package and can't recall who you are. Soon they'll be asking you what time you'd like to come in for an interview. If you'd like, take it a step further and skip the call altogether. Come in for your interview just like that. Chances are you'll get one.

Look at It as an Extra Week of Vacation

When the inevitable batch of rejection letters starts pouring in, don't get too down. There are any number of perfectly good reasons:

1. The personnel director is as lazy as you and sent everybody a form rejection letter.
2. The company combed through thousands of résumés and found that the most qualified applicant was the boss's son-in-law.
3. The ad was a fraudulent offering by someone looking for a good cover letter. Believe it or not, there are people in this world capable of such unethical conduct.

> **R**emember, picking up on the third ring will provide the illusion that you are some ideal combination of busy and alert.

During this period, you may get some phone calls as well. Remember, picking up on the third ring will provide the illusion that you are some ideal combination of busy and alert. When reaching for the receiver, make sure the blender and the erotic cable channel are turned down. And should you decide to rely on an answering machine, erase the gansta-rap-style outgoing message.

The Lazy Person's Guide
to Résumés

Okay, Let's See Some ID

Every job you apply for will require a résumé. Even prisons these days will ask to see a résumé before they invest years of time, space, and resources in some unknown convict. Obviously, then, no matter what you choose to do with your adult years, you will need one of these. As you prepare to write this brief synopsis of your professional life, a voice within you may cry out for complete, unadulterated honesty. This voice should be smothered mercilessly with a sock.

Remember, the résumé is an advertisement for yourself. As in all ads, the gray area between fact and fiction has been widened enough to allow passage for a combine tractor. We have outlined some pointers to help you create that gray area. There is no reason to feel guilty about applying these methods to your product. Everyone is doing it—you might as well do it better. In fact, some folks have ventured clearly over the line, out of the gray area and into the land of fiction and fantasy. Today, these people can generally be found at the top of the corporate ladder. You can, of course, go reasonably far without resorting to any form of lying—as long as a life of servitude at the lower management level suits you.

The Full-Calendar Principle

Dropping the months and days from the start and finish dates of your various jobs can provide the illusion of continuous employment.

Dropping the months and days from the start and finish dates of your various jobs can provide the illusion of continuous employment or, if the interval between jobs was enormous, narrow it. Simply put, which looks better?

Ridgewood Accounting, Clerical Support	Oct. 23, 1987 to March 8, 1988
Bradhurst Real Estate, Clerical Support	Dec. 11, 1988 to July 27, 1989

or

Ridgewood Accounting, Clerical Support	1987–1988
Bradhurst Real Estate, Clerical Support	1988–1989

In accordance with the Full-Calendar Principle, look for jobs toward the end of autumn so that you can quickly get on the books for two distinct calendar years. Theoretically, you could fill in at a gas station every New Year's Eve and with that alone produce the résumé of a modern-day workhorse.

Proliferate Key Verbs

The whole point of a résumé is to demonstrate that you have *done* something with your past, thereby indicating the probability of doing something with your future. Nothing is more effective in propagating this fallacy than the verb. A good verb can give the impression of an intense, driven man or woman on the go. In fact, every sentence in the "accomplishment" section of your résumé should be reworked to begin with a verb in the following fashion:

Incorrect: In-house manual for repair of computer hardware.
Correct: *Prepared* in-house manual for repair of computer hardware.

Not so hard, is it? Just tack that active verb onto the front of that passive noun and you've painted a picture of a low-cost, self-starting dynamo driving the corporate engine into the twenty-first century. Of course, not all verbs are equal. The better the verb you pick, the more impressive you will sound. Verbs can generally be categorized into active, passive, and accurate. For example:

ACTIVE	PASSIVE	ACCURATE
developed	monitored	damaged
performed	served	destroyed
assembled	facilitated	botched
organized	assessed	sabotaged
engineered	reviewed	deleted
designed	streamlined	mangled

Use active verbs wherever possible, use passive verbs if absolutely necessary, and avoid accurate verbs entirely. While honesty may be valuable in an intimate personal relationship, in a résumé it's not worth the hundred percent cotton fiber paper it's printed on.

Explain Away Large Gaps in Employment with "Alternative" Endeavors

What you did with those "lost" years is your business and yours alone. Unfortunately, our intrusive, voyeuristic society seeks to make it everyone else's business as well. You can combat this evil, Orwellian force with the creation of one or more "alternative" endeavors. Perhaps you worked toward a combined MBA and martial arts degree at a little-known one-room school in the Northwest wilderness. Perhaps you developed a program through which wealthy corporate VPs and Hollywood moguls have their leftovers from testimonial banquets and celebrity roasts boxed and delivered to the homeless. Perhaps you served as a decoy in a covert CIA operation to overthrow an unstable, left-leaning Third World government. With the help of a few friends as "references," you should be able to back up any of these unusual endeavors. But whatever you do, don't tell the truth. Following the Grateful Dead around the country in a van for six years may be what "they" wanted to *do,* but it is not what "they" want to *see.*

> Following the Grateful Dead around the country in a van for six years may be what "they" wanted to *do,* but it is not what "they" want to see.

Less Is Better (But You Knew That)

Nothing is more boring than a résumé. It flows about as smoothly as rush-hour traffic and is about as intriguing as a grocery list. Even Madonna's résumé, sexual feats and all, would get boring by the third or fourth page without nude photos. Reading a résumé is painful. Reading many of them is even more painful. Limit your prospective boss's pain by limiting the length of your résumé. She'll appreciate it, and you'll have fewer lies to perpetuate once you start working.

Glamorize Mundane Positions by Rewording

In today's politically correct employment environment, wording is every-thing. The more preposterous, the more commendable. Learn to "translate" your menial old jobs into impressive-sounding former positions. Here are just a few examples:

OLD NAME	NEW NAME
fast food worker	chef
secretary	office-support technician
garbage man	sanitation engineer
taxi driver	human-freight contractor
crossing guard	vehicular-traffic commander
prostitute	licensed libidinal therapist
crook	alternative-morality provider
con artist	attorney

Everybody's doin' it. In fact, calling a job by the same name under which it was known ten or twenty years ago is getting so unusual, your prospective employer might suspect you of making the whole thing up.

The Job Interview: Winning the Guerrilla War

Your Foot, Your Mouth, Your Job

Interviewing is a tricky business. What you say and what you ask during the interview can make or break you. The key is to find out what you need to know without being too revealing about why you need to know it. Sometimes there is a fine line between these two. You can avoid crossing this line with a little common sense. We have included here a sample "Do Say, Don't Say" list as a guide for interviewing. Use it. And although you don't have the job yet, remember: A Freudian slip is like a pink slip.

DO SAY	DON'T SAY
• Do I get a private office?	• Can you hear snoring through the walls?
• Do I get a bonus for completing important, time-sensitive projects early?	• Do I get a bonus for coming in?
• Is there room for promotion?	• Is there room for a bed?
• Who are your competitors?	• Where do I go when I blow this pop stand?
• I like being part of a team.	• I like hiding behind a team.
• Your reputation for consistency and innovation intrigued me.	• This was the only call I got.
• I believe if you work hard, you can get all your important work done by five.	• I'm outta here at five.

- It's important to always be learning something from the job.
- I'm familiar with Windows 95.
- I would like to work with a team leader.
- How do you define your own responsibilities?
- Do you have direct deposit on paychecks?
- Do I get an expense account?

- With how many people would I share support staff?
- Will I get to decorate my own office?
- Does the company provide a connection to the internet?
- When do medical benefits start?

- How long is lunch?

- I'll be winging it.

- I spent '95 looking out a window.
- I would like a team leader to do my work.
- Who are you again?

- Send my first three paychecks to my bookie.
- Is lunch at Hooters considered an expense?
- Do I get the secretary who looks like Pamela Lee?
- Where do I put the VCR?
- Hey, ever checked out the bondage chat room?
- Let's say I have a preexisting condition that might keep me out during summers.
- I think I'm going to lose my lunch. . . .

The Iceberg Principle

Skip stuff like going to the local library to scan business periodicals, running potentially expensive and time-consuming Lexus/Nexus searches, and sending for the company's annual report. Instead, the day of the interview, on your way in, talk to a couple of employees on the periphery. Learn a few interesting facts about the company. For instance, what do they do? Finding out even a few additional little things about the firm—like the names of former senior partners now serving jail time—can only help you. Once you get into the interview, wait for a good chance to work these nuggets of information into the discussion. Think of a convenient segue and go for it.

Now you are in charge of the interview, at least momentarily. You are no longer parrying the interviewer's inquiries, but have free rein to show off your insight and knowledge of the company. Hopefully, the interviewer will think

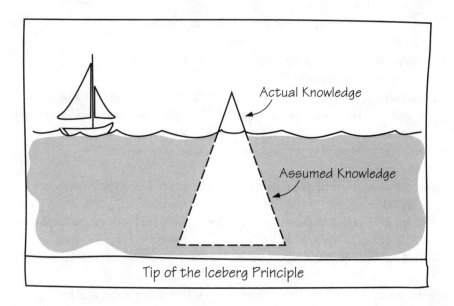

Tip of the Iceberg Principle

that these few fleeting triumphs reveal only the "tip of the iceberg" and that nine-tenths of your knowledge about his company and industry lies below the surface. Little does he know he's already seen the whole iceberg.

"He's Our Man"

The most important objective is to make the interviewer like you. How do you do this? Simple. In fact, the answer is staring you in the face. Look around you at the plaques, trophies, and photographs in his office. Yes, you've always been fascinated by hang gliding. What's it like? No, you're not actually a member of the NRA as he is, but you *have* had your eye on a cute little snubnose revolver at Wal-Mart. And what's that over there? He's kidding you, right? That's him in college? He looks exactly the same today.

Of course, it's always possible that the firm will subject you to an interview (cross-examination?) at some far-off, sterile site, like a conference room. Stripped of all those helpful contextual clues, you will have to find a way to make the interviewer like you based simply on who you are. Good luck.

Eye on the Prize

No matter what garbage happens to come out of your mouth, don't get bogged down mentally by any matter that does not relate directly to getting the job. If you've undertaken the immense bother of actually putting on a suit and interviewing, you owe it to yourself to keep your eye on the prize at hand—booby prize though it may be. Pollyannas still think that interviews represent a sharing of information, where each side can learn more about the other and

> **O**f *course* a fit exists. They have money and you need it.

mutually decide whether a fit exists. Of *course* a fit exists. They have money and you need it.

Another thing. Don't even bother with "exploratory" or "informational" interviews. They're just a waste of time that could be better spent watching reruns of Dr. Bellows being lambasted by General Peterson. The only thing you want to interview for is an actual existing job opening. If you get there and are suddenly told "we don't have any openings at the present time," walk right out. You may still be able to catch the last few minutes of *Montel*.

The Thank-You Note

Skip it altogether. Thank-you notes are for simpering sycophants. They demonstrate an insecurity, specifically that you feel you didn't perform memorably enough during the actual interview and that you now have to go back and jar their memory. No one has ever gotten a job because of a thank-you note. Save them for wedding gifts.

Mulling Over Job Offers

"Civilized" vs. "Sweatshop" Corporations

Once you've received a job offer, take a closer look at the company than the one they probably took at you. Just like people, offices have distinct "personalities." Though probably no large U.S. corporation puts a premium on laziness, there is a wide range of attitudes on work ethic. As a rule, try to avoid companies in hypercompetitive industries. Such corporations tend to believe that the only way to win is to outwork (rather than outthink) the competition. This trend is especially evident in mature industries that specialize in commodities or not-so-glamorous products. While a car may "sell itself," pelletized fertilizer may not. Also avoid financially struggling firms, which try to get away with offering "expanded responsibilities" (that is, more work with longer hours) in lieu of salary increases.

In the erotic toy industry, there's always room at the top.

Good ("civilized") companies to work for, in contrast, are usually found in growing industries, with products that are easily distinguishable from their competition. For instance, if you've seen one brand of acrylic paint, you've seen them all. On the other hand, in the erotic toy industry, there's always room at the top.

Stall for Time!

You don't want to work for a firm that puts pressure on you before you even start working there. Therefore, once you've received an acceptable job offer, let your procrastinating tendencies take over. Don't be in any hurry to accept—thank the person extending the offer and then *stall for time*. Request double the time frame that they first suggest in order to make your decision. Feel free to back down if they take a hard-line stance, but under no circumstances should you agree to make a decision within one week. Two weeks is better. Three weeks gives you enough time to book a lengthy trip to Club Med and still have time left over to procrastinate once you come back.

> **O**nce you've received an acceptable job offer, let your procrastinating tendencies take over.

Once you've decided on a decision date, get going right away on calling in the rest of your cards (well, okay, as soon as *The Rockford Files* is over). Contact your other potential offers and let them know of your need for a speedy decision on *their* part. If more offers do, in fact, come in, play them all against each other, not just for pay and benefits, but for more of that precious decision time. As you approach "stall month" number two, you can afford to have one or more firms drop out of the picture.

Time Off

Don't fall into the trap of accepting *their* labels for time away from the office. Whether they call it "vacation" (which you will take all of), "sick days" (which you will take all of), or "federal holidays" (which you will take all of), the effect is the same—you get paid to stay away. Your bottom line is the sum total of *all* these days offered per year. Also, beware of companies that make you wait six months, a year, or even more before you get to touch the vacation and sick days. If you can't spend a good deal of time on leave the first year, there probably won't be a second year anyway.

> **I**f you can't spend a good deal of time on leave the first year, there probably won't be a second year anyway.

Finally, stay away from companies that openly frown upon using up all your allotted vacation and sick days. Next thing you know, they'll frown upon cashing your entire paycheck.

Sniffing Out Your Potential Boss

Learning about your potential boss is critical when deciding whether or not to accept a job offer. Does he seem "driven to succeed" or "comfortable in his position"? One bad sign is if he is unusually young. In general, the older the boss, the better. A young boss is often a hungry boss, as in hungry for success. And guess who'll be the one to get him there? You got it—you. And you know what that means—work, and lots of it!

Also, a married boss is almost invariably better than a single boss. A married boss will have a spouse to answer to and hence won't be able to live in the office, even if he or she would like to (unless, of course, the spouse is also a rising young professional). A married, older boss with young children is *best* of all. On average, such a boss will not have the freedom or energy to be a workaholic.

The Office

Yet another criterion to consider is the actual office layout. Although there are numerous issues to consider about an office, the key one is "Does it have a door?" A closed (or even ajar) door will provide you with the privacy you need to play computer golf and still have time to recover and "look busy." Also, look around for comfortable furniture like sofas, love seats, and big squishy chairs.

Pseudo Work/Real Work: The Slacker Ratio

> **B**eing tied up by Sharon Stone is qualitatively different from an afternoon of modeling transfer-pricing formulas.

Once you've ascertained the likely work hours and type of boss you'd have, you should turn to the type of work you'd be expected to do. An hour of exotic dancing is not equivalent to an hour of cost accounting. Imagine that Michael Douglas is able to talk about his "work" in much the same way that a company controller talks about his work. Being tied up by Sharon Stone is qualitatively different from an afternoon of modeling transfer-pricing formulas. The higher the slacker ratio, the better.

Fifteen Jobs for the
Truly Lazy

1. **Computer-Games Tester:** Someone has to make sure they work.
2. **Professional Courier:** Free travel, usually no stress, depending, of course, on the nature of what you're couriering. (Bad: organ to be transplanted; anything leaking.)
3. **Musician, Especially Heavy Metal:** Sleep all day; rock all night.
4. **Radiologist:** Keeps banker's hours among usually workaholic physicians.
5. **Toll Collector:** No hard sell involved. Not much selection, either.
6. **Major League Baseball Player:** Average salary of $1 million for playing a "pastime" seven months of the year. Unless you're the pitcher, total time in motion per game is eight minutes.
7. **Tenured Professor:** Lectures a few classes, leaves drudgery of grading and actual teaching to graduate students. Can't be fired, so no need to publish.
8. **Supreme Court Justice:** Good pay; can't be fired. The ultimate sinecure.
9. **Expert Witness:** Tired of actually applying the professional skills he's developed, gives an "opinion" or quick assessment in court regarding what he *would* have done. Typical fee: $500/hour.
10. **Gigolo:** Paid for something he would pretty much do anyway.
11. **Golf Pro:** But what do you do on vacation?
12. **International Spy:** One key strategic secret per year and you're done. Don't get caught, however.
13. **Trashy TV Talk-Show Host:** Pick one line and repeat ad nauseum.

Example: "Don't you realize what you're doing to your family and to yourself?"

14. Paparazzo: One trip per month to Hyannis Port and you're golden.

15. Wine Taster: If only they let you swallow.

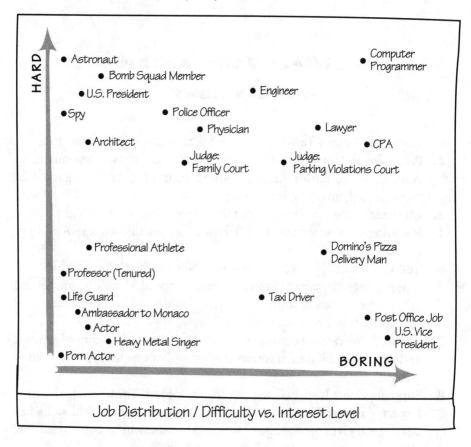

Job Distribution / Difficulty vs. Interest Level

GETTING SETTLED
Life in the Slow Lane

Overcoming Guilt:
The First Day on the Job

The Beast

Look at it this way: The corporation is a Goliath. As the economy blooms and then wilts, Goliath breathes in and breathes out. You are the air that Goliath breathes and needs in order to survive. However, you should understand that *you* are *not* Goliath. The beast himself consists of a select few entrenched high-level executives and large stockholders. They will be cared for no matter what storms or fires ravage the outside environment in which the beast dwells. Under extreme conditions, the beast may even regurgitate to survive, casting out a disbelieving assortment of in-house attorneys, accountants, and VPs that helped line its stomach for so many years. Rest assured that you will be spewed out long before such an event. Therefore, you should clear your mind of any guilt that might keep you from applying the methods in this book to their fullest.

Hello, I Must Be Going

It's your first day on the job. You've gotten a whimsical, irrelevant seven-minute orientation speech from some high-level corporate officer whom you will never again see in this lifetime. From your immediate supervisor, you've gotten a hundred pounds of fat folders you will dump in a corner and leave for good. You've met and shaken hands with the eight or ten people who sit near you and who will be doing most of your work. You've filled your drawers with candy and old stamp-collectors magazines, given your new number to your shrink's secretary, and begun to really settle in at your desk. Your

Guilt and the Lazy

thoughts drift. You look ahead to bigger and brighter things. To an easier life. To quitting in a year or two.

But there's that pang of guilt. Leaving so soon? You just got here! One can dream, can't one? Deep down in the pit of your stomach, you know this is not your destiny. That's the wonderful thing about the mind—it can escape today's prison and enter tomorrow's greener pastures. And where the mind goes, the body is sure to follow, even if it's not immediately.

Small Cog, Big Wheel

The important thing is not to feel guilty about this process. Nowadays, your entire stay can be seen as a transition from the day you accepted your job to the day you quit. Remember: You didn't create this situation—you're simply reacting to it. Time was when being hired by a private firm or a government agency meant acceptance into a family. It was a marriage of sorts, with divorces arising as an exception rather than as a rule, and only when irreconcilable differences arose. You and your family prospered together and suffered together. You gave each other elbow room at the table and kept each other's idiosyncrasies a family secret. When a problem arose, the assumption was always that there was an internal solution, and as a result, there almost always was.

Today, things couldn't be more different. College degree or not, professional expertise or not, intense personal commitment or not, you are a very small cog in a very big wheel. And like that cog, you are highly replaceable, or so your superiors would like you to believe. Analogous to the *factories* of old, today's corporations desire and all too often receive a cheap, endless supply of intellectual labor.

Brains Are Cheap

Why did things change? Essentially, the American economy shifted from being manufacturing-based to being service- and commercial-based. Physical labor was once viewed by the company as the expendable, replaceable commodity, while intellectual labor enjoyed the aura of being lofty, irreplaceable—removed from the unpleasant friction of the daily grind. Today, things are dramatically different. In the final decade of this century, tens of millions of people can read, write, operate computers, answer the phone, and put together spreadsheets. Meanwhile, the number of people who can install a drive shaft is three, and will drop to two in March 1998, when Ernie T. Lewis of Scottsdale, Arizona, retires.

> The number of people who can install a drive shaft is three, and will drop to two in March 1998 when Ernie T. Lewis of Scottsdale, Arizona, retires.

Breezing Through the First Month on the Job: Three Gentle Steps

The first month on the job is the most important and also the most difficult. This is the period when you're being "pegged" by your co-workers and, most importantly, by your boss. And unfortunately, you don't yet know enough about the job to risk cutting too many corners or taking too many liberties. This is the period where "laying low" and feeling out your new environment is critical. But you don't have to impersonate a workaholic to get off to a good start.

> You don't have to impersonate a workaholic to get off to a good start.

1. Establish *Your* Work Hours

A common mistake of the new (but lazy) employee is to impersonate a hard worker by keeping long hours during the first few weeks on the job. Such a strategy may yield short-term benefits, but will only lead to problems in the long run. Let's face facts: As a lazy person, you're eventually going to keep far fewer hours than the average employee. Fortunately, your employer will notice not so much the overall length of your work hours but rather how they *change* over time. So if you start off working much longer hours than everyone else, it's going to be very noticeable once you settle into your usual LIFO routine (see "Who Are the Lazy?"). The boss will think, "What ever happened to Fred? He's really been slacking off lately." Instead, the best strategy is simply to keep the standard operating hours that everyone else does. This way you won't get into any trouble in the short run about being a "slacker," and your eventual slacking off once you get settled in won't be that noticeable a change, either.

2. Act Like You Know What's Going On

Starting any new job is, of course, intrinsically bewildering. You don't know where the copier is, far less all the intimidating new computer systems and office acronyms. Just don't let anyone else in on your confusion. The more you act like you know what's going on, the more people will believe you. Sooner or later you will indeed know what's what, so in the long run, this isn't even a lie. For now, you the lazy person need only to catch on at how to make people *think* you've caught on.

Two simple but critical hints: (1) Keep a running list of office acronyms and interject them whenever and wherever you can, and (2) Make a list of everyone's name. Keep these two lists in easy view on your desk and look them over from time to time. Knowing the names of the people around you will be essential once you're asking them to do your work. Knowing office lingo makes you appear "tapped in," even though you are "tapped out." Both are a heck of a lot easier than actually learning really hard things (like the job's sensational new database software).

3. Be a "Team Player"—But Only for Lunch

One thing an employer will be looking for in a new employee is whether he's a "team player" and "fits in" with the office. The trick is to do as much as you can with others in the office, but not so much that it interferes with your real life outside work. Try occasionally to go out to lunch with people in the office. One-on-one lunches are better than group lunches. Group lunches rarely rise above the "Wow, nobody told me it was blue shirt day!" level of conversation. One-on-one lunches are where you can get the inside scoop, where fellow employees will feel little restraint in letting you know their true feelings about the people around them. Remember, knowledge is power—especially with regard to office gossip. So join the team. You don't have to be the starting shortstop. Even the third-string catcher gets a full World Series share.

Faking the Commute

"How Does He Do It?"

> **P**erhaps more important than actually living close to work is making your fellow employees *think* you live *far* from work.

Naturally, you will want to live close to work, not in order to spend more time at work, but rather to spend less of your life in traffic jams or pressed up against the armpit of a stranger. But perhaps more important than actually living close to work is making your fellow employees *think* you live *far* from work. For the lazy person, this tactic can yield ironclad excuses for everything ranging from occasional lateness to chronic absence.

God Is in the Details

Upon establishing a distant false residency, make sure you spread the word. Everyone from the company president to the guy in the mail room should be

> **C**oming in to work a mere half hour late should be viewed as a magnanimous achievement.

aware of your predicament, your "sacrifice." Coming in to work a mere half hour late should be viewed as a magnanimous achievement. Leaving twenty minutes early should be standard. After all, with your two-and-a-half-hour trip each way, you're either working, traveling, or sleeping. You must really be *dedicated*.

Inevitably, someone will ask you why you don't move closer to work. Perfect time for the tale about the sick uncle you care for, or your asthma that is relieved only by fresh country air. Since you're bound to be asked scores of related questions, be prepared to embellish the saga. This also applies to times when you're not being asked anything and just happen to feel like adding some depth to the picture. Complain about the tie-ups and endless construction along Route 33 (one lane with narrow shoulder). Grumble about your morning bus or train, when possible referring to it by its time of departure: "... the five-thirty-five was late again ...," "... the five-thirty-five was standing room only ...," "... gee, it would be nice to see daylight *just once* while I waited on the platform. ..." Do the same sort of thing in reference to your evening trip.

Appear to be involved with issues germane to your home in the hinterlands: "Wow, with all the rain we've had this year in Catasaqua, that water table's gonna wreak havoc on my septic tank." Or: "Gee, it's a shame they closed the Little League field because of the toxic waste dump." People respect civic concern, and while they are busy admiring it, they will probably fail to spot any inconsistencies in your stories.

Along with the usual signs of hard work, clutter your desk and bulletin board with hometown memorabilia: back issues of the *Catasaqua Gazette*, copies of bills bearing your pseudo address, a framed black-and-white photo of you and someone you will affectionately call the "Mayor." Tell everyone about the time you and the Mayor fell asleep in the fishing boat and sunburned the soles of your feet. Be warned that such heartwarming stories of your pseudo hometown may endear it to your co-workers to the point where they may ask to visit. In that case, be sure to mention the dampness, the fleas, and your crazy Aunt Becky who is convinced the guest room is haunted and performs ritualistic exorcisms there at unannounced times. Any co-worker who still insists on coming probably likes you well enough to be let in on your charade.

Camouflaging the Lazy Person's Office

I Am a Rock, I Am an Island

First off, you want your office to be secluded. Ideally, someone should have to be going to see you exclusively in order to view your office. This setup will minimize the number of visits by your boss or pesky co-workers. Second, having an office with four walls and a door is key—far superior to the rows of space-efficient gray cubicles from which today's star employees are usually harvested. A closed door is your best protection from unscheduled raids by your boss. It affords you the critical few seconds necessary to switch your computer applications from *Mine Sweeper* back to Lotus.

Unfortunately, however, it's becoming politically incorrect to keep your door closed. To do so goes against the "open door" policy many companies now try to maintain. Don't feel shy about breaking with the pack on this one. Your privacy is too important! If your boss remarks about it, just say that the closed door allows you to concentrate better.

Entropy and You

Another trick is to make sure your office looks swamped at all times. Ideally, your desk should look like you've just stepped away in the midst of some incredibly time-sensitive project. This way you can safely maximize the time you spend away from your office, goofing off. For added protection, make sure to take along a clipboard filled with numbers whenever you leave your office. Always have some work on your computer screen. The more compli-cated, the better: Detailed, hard-to-understand spreadsheets probably work best. Or if you have a Windows environment (the Windows computer software, that is, not a window office), be sure to have a number of windows open—as if you're in the midst of "multitasking."

Next, the more cluttered with papers your office is, the busier you look. Having the papers arranged in stacks is critical. Merely scattering them about will not do. Scattered papers suggest disorganization. Stacked papers suggest organized chaos. A calculator, a few stray staples and paper clips, a stapler, some Scotch tape and scissors, along with a strategically placed pair of eyeglasses will round out the organized chaos effect. The glasses suggest that you had to briefly rest your eyes from all your scrutinizing.

Finally, a carefully placed sandwich remnant (preferably still in its wrapper) will do much to enhance the overall ambience of your office. Not only do you appear to eat lunch at your desk, but you also seem to be too busy to finish the remnant or even remember to throw it away. (Be sure to replace with a new, freshly chewed sandwich every few days, though, or co-workers—and insects—may start to catch on.)

> A carefully placed sandwich remnant will do much to enhance the overall ambiance of your office.

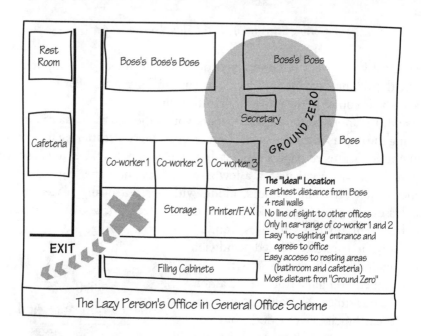

The "Ideal" Location

Farthest distance from Boss
4 real walls
No line of sight to other offices
Only in ear-range of co-worker 1 and 2
Easy "no-sighting" entrance and
    egress to office
Easy access to resting areas
    (bathroom and cafeteria)
Most distant from "Ground Zero"

The Lazy Person's Office in General Office Scheme

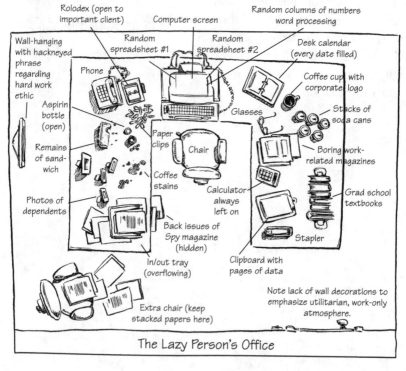

The Lazy Person's Office

Filing Stuff

Trees Are Dying

One thing about work: An insane amount of paper will flow into your office or cubicle, whether you ask for it or not. Very few people read all of it, much less understand all of it. However, most people feel compelled to *file* all of it, thoroughly, into hundreds of separate folders corresponding to a virtually infinite number of categories, subcategories, sub-subcategories, and so on. For example, at your company, you may handle twelve regions, each of which contains anywhere from twenty to a hundred and twenty accounts; each of which requires information on billing, a record of goods or services delivered, a variety of technical information, and endless correspondence. Each of these can be divided further still, many times over. Our advice: Don't bother.

O ur advice: Don't bother.

ABC . . . (Easy as 1, 2, 3)

As a lazy person, you need to surrender to the forces of entropy, scrap the whole concept of "folders," and go with just three piles: need to do something about, *may* need to do something about, and will *never* need to do something about. Can you name anything that *doesn't* fall into one of these three categories? Moreover, your "need" pile will be very small, your "may need" pile perhaps a bit larger, and your "never need" pile will dwarf the other two combined.

Time Management:
Five Strategies

1. That Extra Half Hour

Having an eight-to-five-thirty workday vs. an eight-to-six workday might not seem like much difference. But look at it over the long run. Say you work forty-eight weeks a year, with two weeks off for your personal vacation and two weeks off for holidays. That makes 240 total workdays. Now, if you're able to shave off one-half hour per workday, that results in 120 fewer hours of work per year. Dividing 120 by 8 hours work per day results in the equivalent of 15 fewer workdays (three weeks' worth) per year! Taken over a lifetime, this difference is considerable. Fifteen fewer workdays per year over, say, a 30-year work life results in 450 fewer equivalent workdays, which at 240 total workdays per year results in 1.9 fewer years of work.

> If you're able to shave off one half hour per workday, that results in fifteen fewer workdays per year.

So what is the best method of shaving off that half hour of your workday so that your boss doesn't notice? Some feel that the best strategy is to make sure your boss only overlaps you on one end. For example, if you always come in after your boss, make sure he leaves before you. This way, the reasoning goes, he'll never know just how much later you're working than he is. Since in reality you are leaving just a few minutes after he is, the half hour is made "invisible."

Unfortunately, this strategy doesn't work too well if your boss doesn't arrive or leave at the same time each day. Having to schedule your day around the nuances of your boss's day can quickly grow frustrating. Also, many bosses keep fairly long hours. In such a case it would be quite impractical to overlap him on either side. For these reasons, the most seamless method is to shave fifteen minutes off of either end of your normal workday and hope for the best. Of course, if you're successfully faking the commute, shave at least twice that much off of both ends.

2. The Lunch Break

Another good time to shave additional minutes off your workday is before and after lunch. The strategy resembles that for shaving off the one-half hour of work every day. Just leave for lunch fifteen minutes earlier than everyone else and return fifteen minutes later. If any co-workers notice your absence, they'll most likely think you're in a meeting somewhere or simply not care.

Of course, that doesn't mean that you'll spend all that time eating lunch every day. You can spend perhaps twenty minutes at lunch and then spend the rest of the time running personal errands or getting that skull-and-crossbones tattoo once and for all.

3. One Hour of Personal Stuff per Day

Another professional lazy person's trick of the trade is to bring into the office whatever personal work you have to do. This could include bills to be paid, important phone calls (like to get that "adult" channel added to your cable), correspondence, even job searching. Such personal work is usually pretty well camouflaged by your usual work. Most likely your cable bill looks pretty much like some work-related invoice, so even if your boss should pop in on you, he probably won't notice anything out of the ordinary. Doing a few hours' worth of personal chores at your desk over the course of the normal workweek really opens up cherished free time during the weekend.

4. Four Hours of Productive Output per Day

Studies have shown that the most people can mentally work per day, day in and day out, is between six and seven hours. More than that and one's mind starts to overload and burn out. Much of the time is spent doing pseudo work—organizing their desk, reading nonessential materials, attending meetings, taking coffee breaks, or just plain socializing.

While people may spend many hours at work, that doesn't mean that they're actually *working*.

Once you realize that seven hours' real work per day is about the upper limit over the long term, you can easily see how the lazy person can get by with only four hours of concentrated output per day, if that. The only trick is to make sure those four hours really count. Other folks may work a lot longer and harder, but much of their efforts will be wasted on nonessential activities (activities that in the boss's view don't translate into tangible output). You, in contrast, will make sure that for four hours each day (okay, sometimes every *other* day) you are producing real output, starting with whatever your boss has made top priority.

Look at your workload as an iceberg. Your boss only gets to see the tip of it, but has no way of gauging the ninety percent that lies beneath the surface. Don't waste your time doing the work below the surface—the types of projects that always get put off. The trick is to be constantly aware of your boss's priorities and concentrate solely on completing those projects your boss deems most important. During these four hours of productive output per day, it's key not to allow distractions (people coming by to chat, phone calls, E-mails, etc.) to interfere with your work. Tell people you're "very busy" right now but will get back to them once you're less busy. Such statements also serve to enhance your camouflage as a hard worker.

Right after the snack/newspaper/personal phone call/social rounds ritual, attempt to get some actual work done.

Also, try to get the pain out of the way as quickly as possible. Right after the snack/newspaper/personal phone call/social rounds ritual, attempt to get some actual work done before noon. This way you can enjoy the remainder of your day, knowing that it's going to improve as the day progresses. Then, once you've successfully accomplished your four hours, by all means schmooze with your co-workers. Or better still, finish up that back nine on your computer golf game.

5. The (Dreaded) Crunch Period

Even though you follow these professional lazy person's rules to a tee, certain externalities are going to pop up from time to time to throw you off your gentlemanly game plan. The worst of these is the "Crunch Period." This occurs when your boss hurriedly enters your office and starts describing some important project that needs to be done "at once."

This is the equivalent of a five-alarm fire. But don't panic. Even lazy people are capable of momentary bursts of activity. As Anton Chekhov once observed: "Any fool can handle a crisis. It's the day-to-day living which slowly wears you out."

In fact, in a morbid sort of way, you could relish a Crunch Period. It's a very cost-effective way to maintain or enhance your image in front of your boss. If he

> As Anton Chekhov once observed: "Any fool can handle a crisis. It's the day-to-day living which slowly wears you out."

sees you working assiduously, even staying late (well, no need to get carried away) when something important to him has to be done, he's liable to view your usual relaxed work habits in a more favorable light. That way you'll be better able to maintain your camouflage once your workweek returns to normal.

Sneaking in Some Z's

Opportunity Is Knocking

> **If you come too well-rested for work, you're making a mistake.**

It is important to recognize the many opportunities for catching Z's during office hours. Remember that if you come too well-rested for work, you're making a mistake. Your time outside the office is valuable. Use it. In the morning, when you enter the building, you should feel as if you have just reentered the womb and been embraced by the long, soft arms of the Sandman.

Eureka!

First, we will assume that by sleeping on the job, you are not endangering anyone's safety. For instance, we will assume that you are not an air-traffic controller, and if you are, you either intend to sleep on break only or happen to have an instinctive feel for the airspace while drowsing. Before you snooze, you should quickly review possible defenses in case you are caught. Your most versatile will be the Thomas Alva Edison defense, which has already worked for millions. Inventor Thomas Edison used to place a metal bucket on the floor near his chair and sit with his arm extended, holding a metal spoon out over the bucket. He claimed that his best ideas for inventions came during short episodes of sleep, and that he could best remember those ideas by awaking quickly. As he lost control of his body, the spoon would drop into the bucket, wake him up, and *violà*—the phonograph!

You can follow in the great inventor's footsteps, albeit at a somewhat slower pace. Bring a bucket and a spoon in to work. Place the spoon in the bucket and the bucket on the floor. If you are caught napping, no problem. You were in deep sleep trying to figure out why your company lost $125 million last quarter. You were so concerned, as indicated by the depth of your slumber, that even Mr. Edison's gong couldn't bring you to. When sleeping on the job, it's also a good idea to keep a recently completed report on the computer screen or at arm's reach. This way, when you are roused, you can declare: "Good timing, Mr. Johnstone, I just finished *this*." You can probably use the same report over and over again.

> You were in deep sleep trying to figure out why your company lost $125 million last quarter.

Naturally, you'd rather not get caught napping in the first place; getting caught should be the exception rather than the rule. A good investment is a five- or ten-dollar digital watch with an alarm clock function. Predetermine your naps for twenty or thirty minutes and you may never have to rely on Mr. Edison. Random incoming phone calls provide a logical terminus to a nap as well.

Desktop Kama Sutra

It is also useful to review the four basic positions for desk slumber:

1. Position number one entails simply placing your head in one hand, and the elbow of the same arm on the desktop. This is ideal for very brief naps, since you will probably lose balance only moments after nodding out. This position is also ideal for keeping marginally aware of people entering your work area, enabling you to snap out of it just when you need to.

2. Position number two is a variation of number one, wherein your dozing head is supported by both hands and both elbows. This position will provide a bit more structural stability for a slightly longer nap. By

covering both eyes, it will make you less aware of your surroundings, but by the same token will allow you to claim your eyes were never actually closed.

3. Position number three involves simply leaning back in your chair and closing your eyes. For added stability, you can use a back wall to brace your head. Should someone walk into your space, it will likely be obvious that your eyes were closed, but there is a certain dignity that comes with honesty. Like a Zen master, you were meditating to achieve peace and harmony, so as to bolster your firm's position on the *Fortune 500*. Ask Ms. Rise and Shine if *she* has meditated for the good of the company, and if not, *why* not.

> Ask Ms. Rise-and-Shine if *she* has meditated for the good of the company, and if not, *why* not.

4. Position number four requires a full-fledged commitment to sleep: head down on your desk with arms and hands in cradling formation. While this will enable a nice long dance with the angels, it increases your chances of getting caught proportionately. Fortunately, the position suggests complete exhaustion (from work, of course), which is what you'll have to claim.

Don't Be Coy

Choosing to sleep outside the office is often your best bet for uninterrupted, guilt-free slumber. Lunch is an obvious time for this, as is when you offer to deliver a package. If you choose a park or a public plaza for your mini-vacation, make sure it's off the beaten path of your boss and co-workers. A library is also good for extra-office slumber, as is a massage table in the back of a health club. Make sure these facilities, too, are not normally frequented by people from your company.

Catching Z's during meetings may be risky to your reputation. However, it *will* make meetings go faster and may be contagious to the point where no one will remain awake to catch you in the act. To be on the safe side, keep naps during meetings *very* brief, like twenty or thirty seconds. Believe it or not, this can be refreshing. When the CEO's statements on "diminishing marginal

The Big Sleep

utility in a shrinking market" become thoughts of assuming a fetal position and eating Milk Duds, you know it's time to open your eyes.

The Big Sleep

Occasionally, you might want to pull out all the stops and go for an in-office, open-ended sleep, perhaps having recently completed a big assignment. Close and lock your door if you have one. Forward all calls to voice mail. Turn off your beeper. Grab something resembling a pillow and curl up on the floor of your room. While this may represent a high point of your career and leave you feeling great about life, let's hope that during sleep you are sensitive to sirens and to fists furiously pounding on your door in the event of a fire.

> If you find yourself dreaming about office situations, you need to seek professional help immediately.

One final note: Sleep is supposed to be an escape. It certainly shouldn't plunk you back into the office. If you find yourself dreaming about office situations, you need to seek professional help immediately.

Eight Golden Rules of
Office Life

Now that you've awoken from your office nap, time to get back to work. Not. Better to pick up a few tips that will help you get through the rest of the day—and all the days that follow—with minimal effort.

1. The Buck Does Not Stop Here

This is not 1949, and you are not Harry Truman. The notion that there is a person at the end of the line who is ultimately responsible for and answerable to all the errors, oversights, and evasions that preceded him is certainly a comforting one—as long as that person is not you. Such a person is likely to possess a mammoth ego, an iron constitution, and a tireless will. Not only does this *not* describe you, it doesn't even describe someone you could *portray* for a few minutes in a TV miniseries. If you're in the buck-stopping business, get out. If you are already out, *stay* out.

2. Know When to Shut Up

Sometimes you find yourself in an odd position. Two or more people who have it in for each other are about to come to verbal blows and you are in the room. To the untrained ear, they seem to be arguing about whether to go with a 16 MByte or 32 MByte RAM. But you know better. You know these two simply don't like each other. Overcome the temptation to intercede. *Megabyte your lip.* Virtually whatever you say will be wrong, not because you lack solutions or social skills, but because nobody loves the referee. In fact, referees get punched out when they're in the way. In this volatile world of interpersonal chemistry, stay out of the water until acid and base have reacted thoroughly and the pH is back to normal.

3. One Good Memo Deserves Another

Somewhere in the world, there are people actually hammering nails into wood, hauling earth from one place to another, rebuilding six-cylinder engines, and harvesting numerous acres of grain. God bless them. We all need homes, transportation, and something to eat. However, the rest of us are content merely to discuss, document, and "manage" such noble efforts. A good rule of thumb is this: The greater the physical, emotional, or spiritual distance from which you discuss, document, or manage these efforts, the greater will be your value and reward, both in your company and your society. And that leads us to memos. Someone, somewhere will write you a memo regarding a real problem with real causes and real symptoms. If you respond to that memo with real action, you have fallen into the trap. Yes, the copier is broken. But fixing it yourself might take you away from the *Sports Illustrated* Web site. Worse yet, while performing genuine and direct labor,

One Good Memo Deserves Another

Why not shoot back a memo "analyzing" the problem one degree further?

you will have unwittingly taken yourself down a couple of notches in the pecking order. Instead, why not shoot back a memo "analyzing" the problem one degree further? Or ignore the original memo completely.

4. Avoid Finishing Other People's Sentences

We understand the impulse. You want to show people how in tune you are with their thoughts. But if you really *were* in tune with their thoughts, you'd know how much they love to hear themselves speak. From singing in the shower to leaving long-winded messages on your answering machine to saying the same thing five different ways during a meeting, people can't seem to get enough of themselves. If you're smart, you'll let them try. If you feel the need to let the other person know you're still awake, a simple, sporadic "Uh-huh" or "Right" will do. You'll be rewarded with a reputation as someone who not only listens but who also understands, even though you probably don't. Avoid trouble, hard unnecessary work, and embarrassment—don't go through life like a trigger-happy contestant on *Jeopardy*.

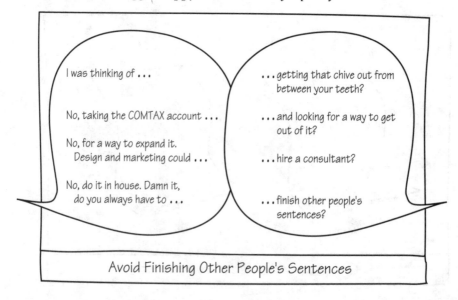

I was thinking of . . .

. . . getting that chive out from between your teeth?

No, taking the COMTAX account . . .

. . . and looking for a way to get out of it?

No, for a way to expand it. Design and marketing could . . .

. . . hire a consultant?

No, do it in house. Damn it, do you always have to . . .

. . . finish other people's sentences?

Avoid Finishing Other People's Sentences

5. A = mc²: The Lazy Person's Theory of Sensitivity

Aggravation equals mental effort, multiplied by concern squared. While Einstein's theory of relativity ($E = mc^2$) unlocked the power of the atom, redefined global politics, and altered the way human beings view existence itself, the Lazy Person's Theory of Sensitivity has had a truly important impact—that of minimizing grief in the workplace. Think about it: Aggravation—that gut-wrenching, mind-throbbing feeling of helplessness—has two distinct and necessary components: mental effort and concern. Alone, mental effort may make you tired, but will not aggravate you. Similarly, concern alone may lead to emotional involvement but not aggravation.

Rather, it is the insidious combination of mental effort *and* concern that will invariably lead to aggravation. Remember, *a project at work* is just that; make sure you *leave* it at work. And even while you are at work, keep your emotional distance. The odds are one in a million at best that the project will have a direct bearing on you or anyone you know in the outside world. If you find, however, that you cannot humanly avoid giving a damn, try not to work too hard or at all on the project. Getting transferred to another assignment is one potential solution. Being your old lazy self is another option. If you neglect the equation, the first serious roadblock you hit will produce the tumor we call aggravation. Left unchecked, that tumor may grow quickly and spell your downfall. In any case, if you can't lick both components, focus on licking one. And watch out in particular for concern—it's squared.

6. Invent an Easily Solved Problem

Everyone from the president of the United States on down to someone pumping frozen yogurt in the mall feels compelled to justify his or her existence. The mall employee may argue that he provides a tasty, nutritious, relatively low-calorie treat at a reasonable cost to hundreds of hungry customers each day. There are more complicated, perhaps less plausible or compelling justifications for the president's existence.

You were born with the self-justification compulsion, too, but alas, you are lazy. Therefore, your best bet is to invent an easily solved problem and solve it, rather than find a real and intractable one out there in the cold, cruel world. What is something that by accident or by mindless trial and error you already know? Perhaps it's how to change the margins on a computer document

Forget the sneaker commercial: *Don't* just do it.

you've prepared. Or how to acquire census information for a target market. Forget the sneaker commercial: *Don't* just do it! Make a plea to your boss for help, but "solve" the problem before she has a full chance to respond. In this manner, you will build a reputation as a resourceful self-starter while expending minimal effort. While neatly filling in blanks you yourself have created, you will be seen as an ad-libber extraordinaire. In the chain store operation called life, you will be regarded as a successful franchise operator.

7. Don't Make Waves

Unless you are at the beach or a ball game, forget about making waves.

Unless you are at the beach or at a ball game, forget about making waves. At the beach, you can ride one. At a ball game, you can participate in one. At the office, you will drown in one. There are always exceptions, but make sure you have a powerful stroke before you risk sucking in a lungful of H_2O. When we say "lay low," we mean on land—not at the bottom of the sea.

8. Make Them Think You Have Standing Offers Elsewhere

You will never be more valuable in the eyes of your supervisors and co-workers than when you leave voluntarily. That is why you must *always* appear to be leaving or at least considering it. Your potential status as a former employee will bring you more in the way of raises, promotions, and respect than hard work ever will. Sprinkle your conversations at work liberally with subtle allusions to your clandestine job search: "You know, Bob, until a couple of days ago, I had no idea what I was *worth*." On at least one occasion, slam the phone down when someone from the office nears your desk. As someone who seems to be moving on to bigger and better things (that is, *anything*), you will be revered by co-workers as never before.

And don't be surprised if your efforts culminate in a meeting with upper-level management at which your company offers to match any counteroffers.

GETTING THE BEST . . .
Out of Others

Managing the Boss
Made Easy

Lay (You Got It) Low

Hillel was once asked to summarize the entire Bible while standing on one foot. "Do not do unto others," he replied with one foot on the ground, "as you would not have done unto you." Well, now it's our turn to stand on one foot: Where possible, avoid high-exposure projects! If you should have the misfortune of getting such a project, one of two unpleasant scenarios will occur: (1) You screw it up (that is, you make the big mistake), or (2) You do a bang-up job.

Heads I Win . . .

The consequences of the first outcome are immediately obvious. You screw up and you end up in the doghouse. But the second outcome is even worse than the first. Now that you're recognized as a high achiever, you're going to be first in line for similar projects. Your cover is blown. Soon a torrent of these "high-exposure" projects will come your way, a veritable missile barrage on your lifestyle.

. . . Tails You Lose

And then what eventually happens? You screw up. It's inevitable; if you keep getting put on high-exposure projects, you'll eventually make a mistake. Except this mistake will not be an ordinary mistake—no, it'll be (you guessed it) the big mistake. Then you're right back where you would have been had you screwed up to begin with—in the doghouse. Except in the interim, your lifestyle has also suffered a horrific hit as you race through one high-exposure assignment after another. Win the war of attrition: let all the high fliers soar and then inevitably get shot down back to earth. You, meanwhile, will just keep gliding through the job and steadily advancing your career.

> **W**in the war of attrition: let all the high flyers soar and then inevitably get shot back down to earth.

Damage Control

Despite your vigilance, however, every now and then you're going to make a mistake that is noticed. In these cases, be sure to minimize your losses. Everyone will run into some trouble with his boss from time to time. Where you'll set yourself apart, however, is how you respond to the attack. The following are two handy hints:

1. Don't argue with your boss—agree with her! This is a classic preemptive manuever. Before she gets all worked up, say something like, "You're right, it's clear I haven't done a good job at this. Looks like I'll have to go back and get it right." You'll be denying her her thunder and, more importantly, will make it appear that you are your own worst critic—even tougher on you than she is!

2. Make allusions to your heavy workload, without using it as a direct excuse. Just saying something like, "Yeah, I guess I was so busy with Project X that that item on Project Y skipped my eye." This way you won't be labeled as a malingerer, but the critical seed will be planted: "I better not load him down much more, or he's liable to make similar mistakes."

Managing the Boss Made Easy: Advanced Methods

1. Ingratiate Yourself with the Boss's Spouse or Partner

Strike up conversations with the boss's spouse/partner at office parties. Pretend to be wholly interested in even the most mundane accounts of domestic life, like how the azaleas are wilting this year. Afterward, when the debriefing occurs, the spouse/partner will be sure to mention how "entertaining" or "charming" you were. A classic encirclement maneuver.

2. Talk About His Interests

Learn what his top interests are (if any) outside of work. Then look for opportunities to steer chitchat to those subjects. This will make him think you're as interesting as he thinks he is. Pretend to be wholly interested in even the most mundane accounts of domestic life, like how when he's too lazy to walk the dog, he lets him go in the azaleas.

3. Compliment Your Co-workers in His Presence

This pegs you as a "team player." However, avoid complimenting people you've heard he despises.

4. Bring Her Little Newspaper Articles Relating to Work

The boss will think you really live for this stuff. But make sure you've read them yourself, in case she ever brings one up in conversation. Unless they

Keep Her Well-Fed with Company Gossip

seem particularly apropos, avoid articles from *The Star, The Globe,* and *The National Enquirer.*

5. Keep Her Well Fed with Company Gossip

This strategy satisfies her natural appetite for gossip and makes her think you're well connected in the corporate bureaucracy. However, in keeping with Tactic 3, keep the gossip generally on the neutral side, at least until you know her well enough to distinguish between her friends and enemies.

6. Laugh at Her Jokes, No Matter How Pitiful

We all like to think we've got a great sense of humor. So when she tells you how many Jewish grandmothers it takes to screw in a light bulb ("None, I'll just sit here in the dark") or some other overused joke that should have been allowed to die in peace ten years ago, burst out laughing. Of course, this is not so easy. As Lenny Bruce once said, nothing is harder to fake than a laugh—except perhaps a paycheck. So give it the old college try.

7. Be Sure to Maintain a Steady Work Output Flow

Even if you're working on a lengthy long-term project, be sure to provide the boss with a steady dose of output showing "progress." This will demonstrate that you're approaching the project in the way she sees fit. She'll also unconsciously believe that you're churning out a lot more work than you really are. Ten little projectettes give the impression of a lot more work than does one megaproject.

8. Warehouse a Few Non-Time-Sensitive Projects for a Rainy (or Particularly Lazy) Day

Don't be in a hurry to hand over non-time-sensitive projects. Instead, hold on to them until sometime when you *especially* don't feel like working.

9. Ambush Him

As long as you can be "on" when in front of your boss, it doesn't matter how brain-dead you are for the rest of the day. Look upon it as guerrilla warfare. Perform well in brief hit-and-run episodes and then disappear back into the bush.

A Field Guide to Bosses

Not all bosses should be handled alike. Adjust your boss-management strategies to suit your particular boss's nature. Determining his true nature is half the battle. Following are seven subspecies of boss that you're likely to run into in your career and how to approach and (if possible) tame them:

The Charioteer

Behavior in Corporate Jungle: Whips his employees mercilessly in order to get ahead (also his fellow managers when others aren't looking). A classic sycophant-sadist. Shamelessly kisses up to superiors. Viciously tortures subordinates. *Recognizable Features & Other Markings:* Index finger pointed at underlings. *Typical Vocalization:* "Why isn't the revision finished yet?" *How to Handle:* Reduce efforts to MAP (minimal acceptable performance), as he'll never be satisfied anyway, and look for a new job.

The Boofus

Behavior in Corporate Jungle: Incompetent. Got into current position through smoke and mirrors or "connections." *Recognizable Features & Other Markings:* Faintly glazed-over look. *Typical Vocalization:* "Uh-huh. Yeah, I understand. Uh-huh." *How to Handle:* Carefully. Don't tease him or he may turn vicious. Bring him food to appease him if necessary. Bail him out of a few tight spots resulting from his being mentally overmatched. Like a lion from whose paw you have removed a thorn, he will be your friend evermore.

Mr. Meek

Behavior in Corporate Jungle: Holds the position as boss, but lacks the psychology for the job. Often seeks acceptance from his subordinates. *Recognizable Features & Other Markings:* Too shy to look employees in the eye or issue direct orders. *Typical Vocalization:* "Would it be okay if you did this project for me? I mean if you're not too busy." *How to Handle:* Always be too busy for labor-intensive, high-exposure projects. Milk this arrangement for what it's worth and while it lasts.

The Little Napoleon

Behavior in Corporate Jungle: Commands his subordinates. Not to be confused with the Charioteer, the Little Napoleon has too many ego concerns and leadership illusions to spend much time browbeating any particular individual. *Recognizable Features & Other Markings:* Refers to his subordinates as his "troops." *Typical Vocalization:* "All right, troops, we're going to need a big effort over these next few weeks." *How to Handle:* Play the good soldier, but don't volunteer for any extra duty. Salute if necessary. Issue him periodic "reports from the front." Earn your purple heart. Become a casualty once in a while by calling in sick.

The Favoritist

Behavior in Corporate Jungle: Indiscriminately favors certain subordinates over others. The chosen ones enjoy a bed of roses; the "unchosen" get a bed of nails. *Recognizable Features & Other Markings:* Chummy with some subordinates; petty and businesslike with others. *Typical Vocalization:* "How 'bout them Cowboys!" or "Why isn't the XMX151 request completed yet?" depending on to whom she is speaking. *How to Handle:* If not one of the chosen ones, look for another job or a transfer. If chosen, milk it.

The Do-It-Herself

Behavior in Corporate Jungle: Only trusts herself to get things done right. Hence, her employees do only the most routine of tasks (those not even they could screw up). *Recognizable Features & Other Markings:* Constantly working. *Typical Vocalization:* "Just let me do it." *How to Handle:* Let her do it.

The Anal-Retentive

Behavior in Corporate Jungle: Super-detail-oriented. *Recognizable Features & Other Markings:* More concerned with a report's margins and font than content. Files things alphabetically by folder, *chronologically* within folder. Makes backups of backups. Issues memos summarizing your work-related discussions. *Typical Vocalization:* "Is that in Helvetica twelve-point?" *How to Handle:* Make sure things are in Helvetica twelve-point.

Good Boss/Bad Boss Traits

Good Boss Traits

- Married (especially if spouse doesn't work).
- Has children (especially young ones).
- Fantasizes about being a house-husband (or wife).
- Over fifty.
- Doesn't conduct bed checks of employees' comings and goings.
- Well-versed in early-evening TV lineups. Can name three or more characters each from *Seinfeld* or *Friends*.
- Exudes overall live-and-let-live attitude.
- Takes his own boss with a grain of salt (or a shot of whiskey).
- Has some sort of secret artistic life.
- Believes he has "peaked" where he is and isn't frustrated by that.

Bad Boss Traits

- Uses words "work" and "night" in same sentence.
- Routinely gets in before official starting time.
- Routinely leaves after official quitting time.
- Eats breakfast at desk.
- Eats lunch at desk.
- Eats dinner at desk.
- Calls the CEO "The Chairman" or "Mr.——" instead of by his last name.
- Fawns over his boss.

- Talks a lot about "exposure."
- Refers to his employees as "resource" (as in "We'll throw more resource at the project").
- Shooting for CEO himself.
- Leaves "Please See Me" notes on your chair every morning before you arrive.
- Compares his employees' work ethic with his own.
- Majored in business in college and graduate school.

How to Handle Meetings Without Preparation or Concentration

Given the tedium of office meetings and all the fun things in the world to daydream about instead, one of the toughest tasks for the lazy person in such situations is to keep his concentration. This chapter will help the lazy person excel in business meetings while minimizing the need to pay attention or, worse yet, prepare for them.

Conduct a Guerrilla War

In much the same way you engage in guerrilla warfare with your boss, you can play hit-and-run at a meeting. By doing so, you will be able to minimize your attention span and emerge completely or relatively unscathed. As in any guerrilla war, the trick is to pick your spots. For example, even by paying just the scantiest attention to the discussion, you should be able to pick out at least one instance per meeting where something patently ridiculous is stated. That is your moment to leap into action. Politely and affably point out the flaw in that person's line of reasoning and then blend back into the corporate jungle. For instance: "Tom, you should know, we no longer *compete* with NBC—we *own* it." As the commanding officers perform a body count, you can begin camouflage operations for your next ambush.

> You can play hit-and-run at a meeting.

The Importance of Facial Gesturing

Even if you don't know (or care to know) about what's going on during a particular meeting, you can affect the appearance of being on top of things just by interjecting the proper facial mannerism at the right moment. Often all that's required is that you mimic the responses of everyone else around you. For example, if someone says something others regard as funny, smile and shake your head wryly. If someone says something regarded as troubling, frown slightly. If not sure how to react, just look mildly pensive. If nodding your head will keep you from nodding off, by all means do so. An occasional "Hmm" or "Whew" in the right place can go a long way as well. With some luck, by the end of the meeting, though you won't have said or understood anything, the impression will be that you were a full participant.

If not sure how to react, just look mildly pensive.

A Few Pointers for "Sounding" Intelligent

Another weapon in your arsenal for scraping through meetings without extending yourself is to sound intelligent whenever you do speak up or (worse yet) are called upon to say something. Remember, in the corporate meeting image is everything. Here are a few hints that should come in handy with your image management:

- **Be sure to pepper your observations with key words** and catch-phrases that sound thoughtful and intelligent (see "Glossary of Key Words and Catchphrases to Impress Folks in Business Meetings," which follows this list).
- **Sound gruff.** For some reason people with gruff-sounding voices seem to carry more weight than those with higher-pitched voices. Observe Marlon Brando in *The Godfather*.
- **Stare off into space while making your point,** then look someone straight in the eye when you conclude it. This technique makes you look both thoughtful and then direct and confident in turn.

- **Use acronyms wherever possible.** Using acronyms makes people think you know the material cold.
- **Build on what someone else said.** This is especially useful when that person is someone above you whom you'd like to impress and whom others respect. For instance: "What Steve said about print advertising is right on the money. But I'd like to take it a step further. I think it's clear that what he said now applies to *all* forms of advertising!"
- **Be "in tune."** Tentatively raise and then quickly lower your hand as someone else begins making what obviously will be a good point. When people ask you what it was you had to say, respond: "I was about to make the exact same point."
- **Reword a good point** someone made an hour earlier in the meeting. Chances are no one will recognize it.

Glossary of Key Words and Catchphrases to Impress Folks in Business Meetings

Autocorrelation and Multicollinearity (*nouns*) Real technical terms dealing with statistical analysis. Autocorrelation refers to the relationship between successive errors (determined by the rarefied "Durban-Watson Statistic"), while multicollinearity refers to the correlation between two or more independent variables. (It's really not that necessary to actually know what they mean, just that you interject one or both should a statistical discussion come up. You'll always sound intelligent by throwing in these two terms when discussing regressions.) "Did you check for multicollinearity and autocorrelation?"

Indifference Curve (*noun*) Fancy way of saying it makes no difference. "Frankly, those two options reside on the exact same indifference curve for me."

Lean and Mean (*adjective*) Modern alternative to plump and kind.

Learning Curve (*noun*) How long it will take in order to get really good at something. "It could take weeks for our sales force to work their way up their learning curve."

Marginal Return (*noun*) How much output you get for just a little more input. Overlaps other terms in glossary, but is a winner nonetheless. "Coming in to work an hour early every day *sounds* nice, but what is the *marginal return?*"

Mutually Exclusive (*adjective*) Fancy way of saying you can have one but not the other. "It appears to me that buying and selling are mutually exclusive. So let's decide on the best one today and get it over with."

Paradigm Shift (*noun*) New Age term for looking at things in a totally new way. "I think we've been looking at things all wrong. I suggest a paradigm shift in the way we go about our business."

Patently (*adverb*) Synonym for "clearly" or "obviously." As in, "Such a statement is patently ridiculous. Have you ever considered what such a cost-cutting maneuver will do to our product quality and premium image?"

Resource (*noun*) Business term for "people." As in, "Is it really worth devoting so much resource on a project that offers such a minimal return?"

Risk-Return Trade-off (*noun*) Another way of saying how risky something is compared to the expected upside potential. "It seems to me that such a strategy represents a meager risk-return trade-off."

Sensitivity Analysis (*noun*) The range of best, average, and worst expected outcomes. "It would be prudent to conduct some sensitivity analysis on this strategy before committing ourselves to it."

Specious (*adjective*) Referring to an argument or line of reasoning that sounds good at first, but then becomes preposterous when examined a bit further. "Your idea to increase revenue by raising prices is specious when you consider our product faces a highly elastic demand curve."

Streamlining (*noun*) Downsizing. But downsizing is a dirty word.

Top-Heavy (*adjective*) 1. Too many chiefs, not enough Indians. 2. A quick, effortless way of appearing to have done an in-depth organizational analysis. (Make sure no one in the room is at the top, heavy, or both.)

WSJ (*noun*) Acronym for the *Wall Street Journal*. "I just read an article in last Tuesday's *WSJ* on just that subject." When the acronym has more syllables than the phrase it represents, people will really respect you.

A Field Guide to
Office Co-workers

During your career in the big company, you the lazy person will encounter a wide variety of corporate fauna. The following serves as a handy field guide while prowling the corporate jungle:

The Shield

The Shield is a, how shall we say, less than competent co-worker. An essential component for any lazy person's work group, the Shield screws up a lot, maintains uneven work hours, and is generally unreliable. He takes the brunt of the boss's scorn, thus shielding the lazy person and helping him to Lay Low and Not Make the Big Mistake. *Vocalization:* I can't believe I did that! *Dangerous?* Quite the opposite.

The Amiable Geek/Office Drone

This species vocalizes incessantly on work-related minutiae, which serves as its equivalent for conversation. *Vocalization:* "Did you notice that Empire-Phillips' total sales volume was up three-point-five percent last quarter, yet its profit margin actually rose only a half point? Pretty scary stuff." *Dangerous?* Not usually, unless it exposes the lazy person's camouflage of not being particularly interested in the workload. She is best indulged with a nod and a "Hmmm, interesting . . ."

The Workaholic

Lives for work. Avoids vacations. Thinks Jessie Jackson was in the Jackson 5. *Vocalization:* "I can't talk to you right now. How about trying back next Thursday after six?" *Dangerous?* Potentially, especially if he serves to flush the lazy person out of his cover. He is best handled by letting him work to his heart's content on behalf of the both of you.

The Curmudgeon

Constantly grumbling about petty office outrages. *Vocalization:* "Can you believe this new office policy? Now they want us to recycle our paper? What is this, the World Wildlife Federation?" *Dangerous?* No. Maintains symbiotic relationship with lazy person. Helps lazy person maintain his cover.

The Bitter, Spinster, Evil-Genius Secretary

Could have amounted to something and knows it. Now reduced to petty backbiting and general unpleasantness. Untrustworthy and lives for stirring up office gossip and turmoil. *Vocalization:* "Xerox it yourself." *Dangerous?* Potentially. The lazy person must take special care to stay on her less bad side.

The Teacher's Pet

The boss's favorite. Ingratiating, untrustworthy, and uninteresting. *Vocalization:* "Do you need me to come in this weekend?" *Dangerous?* Very. Keen to foul lazy person's habitat.

The Freak/Eccentric

Had an interesting life in the past and pathetically flaunts it. Now just another subspecies of Amiable Geek/Office Drone. *Vocalization:* "Hey, man, this new update of Lotus is totally rad!" Usually harmless—but watch out for the odd LSD flashback. Not indigenous to the corporate environment, but a transplanted organism thrown in by some twist of fate. *Dangerous?* No. Enhances general office environment while serving to further camouflage the lazy person.

The Old-timer

A survivor in the corporate jungle. Has seen it all and calls upon well-honed survival instincts to scrape by another business cycle. *Vocalization:* "Three more years till my pension kicks in." *Dangerous?* Innocuous.

The Backstabber

The Great White Shark of the office environment. *Vocalization:* "Oh, finally back from lunch? I was hoping to get that report back from you, but when I asked (insert boss's name), he said he had no idea where you were. By the way, what time are you planning on leaving today?" *Dangerous?* A bloodthirsty carnivore that feeds on co-workers. Avoid at all costs.

The Good Soldier

Hardworking and amiable. Ex-military, does whatever is needed to get the job done, and has a very high threshold for pain. *Vocalization:* "Darn, that electrical outage just destroyed five hours of work. That'll teach me for not backing up my work every fifteen minutes. Looks like I'll just have to stay till 0100 to finish it." *Dangerous?* Usually innocuous, unless directly compared to lazy person by boss.

Choose Your Teammates Wisely

I Love This Game

Remember Ernie Banks? He played shortstop and first base for the Chicago Cubs for nineteen years. He came to the ballpark to play hard every day. By the time he was finished, he had amassed over 500 home runs and 1,600 RBI. And in all that time, with all that work, did he win even one World Series or pennant? No.

Remember Phil Jackson? He played basketball for the New York Knicks for a few years in the late sixties to mid-seventies. He was surrounded by great players like Walt Frazier, Willis Reed, Dave DeBusschere, and Bill Bradley (a real workaholic). Phil Jackson himself was the "eleventh man," coming in for a few minutes each game to pull down a rebound or two and give someone an elbow. He reached the championship three times in the space of four years and came away with championship rings in 1970 and 1973. Later in life, he "coached" Michael Jordan and Scottie Pippen and found himself with four more championship rings. What's the lesson here? Choose your teammates wisely!

Dream Team

Where a project is involved and you *have* such a choice, make it work for you. Putting six or seven type-A personalities (workaholics) together in a room may not produce the best report, regardless of how knowledgeable each participant claims to be or how much work each is willing to take home over the weekend. Okay, it probably *will* produce the best report. This is the kind of project team you want to be on, with one condition—that *you* be the person responsible for reporting the group's progress to the higher-ups. There will not be much else for you to do. Other team members will be so eager to get your attention, it will appear that you are an integral part of the operation.

Be kind to your intense, driven teammates, lavishing praise on their work. Appear to rise and fall emotionally with their triumphs and failures. When reporting orally or in writing to upper management, use the word "we" liberally and lavish praise some more. If there was a small problem, take most of the responsibility yourself. Your teammates will love you for it and upper management will assume you were selflessly covering for someone else.

> **B**e kind to your intense, driven teammates, lavishing praise on their work.

Above all else remember this: The mark of a good team player is that he knows when to let himself be carried. In your case, this will be as often as possible. Surf's up!

Moving Up in the Company—The Joy of Delegation

The Ladder

This isn't merely a "How to Slide By" book but, for those who seek such fortunes, a book on how to *succeed* in the corporate world. Having read, skimmed, or even casually flipped through to this section, you may be ready for the next step—getting promoted. Many lazy people are understandably anxious about the idea of being promoted. After all, since they're getting paid more and have added responsibilities, aren't they expected to work even harder? The answer is not necessarily. For with promotions comes the ability to delegate.

The Less They Know

The trick to successful delegating is to balance the workload on your subordinates so that no one of them is particularly abused. Of course, there are those employees who are happiest when they've got lots of work to do, especially if such work will provide them with lots of "exposure." So for those employees, by all means make 'em happy!

> **The beauty of delegation is that none of your employees will realize how little work you have.**

The beauty of delegation is that none of your employees will realize how little work you have. They'll just assume you have lots to do. Your own boss is going to be concerned with your group's output, not with *how* this output is achieved. If you get really good at delegating, you'll become just a work coordinator without having to do any of that nitty-gritty real work yourself. And if you get *really* good at coordinating, you'll be promoted again, thereby becoming a coordinator of coordinators and doing less real work than ever before. Should this process continue a few more levels, you will find yourself the leader of a large company or government agency, having only to make three or four crucial decisions per year, each of which can be determined reasonably by a coin toss.

"HEADS WE GO PUBLIC..."

Life at the Top

A Mercifully Short Course
in Management

Some Teach Gym

There's an old joke that goes something like this: A group of people get shipwrecked on a desert island. It appears they may be stranded for some time. On his deathbed, the captain of the ship interviews his passengers one by one. "What do you do?" he asks the first one. "I'm a carpenter," the man replies. "Okay, start gathering wood and building huts. What do you do?" he asks the next one. "I'm a physician," the woman replies. "Fine," the captain asserts, "start bandaging the wounded. What do you do?" he asks the third one. "I'm a farmer," the man responds. "Then clear a field and start planting crops," the dying captain instructs. Finally, the dying captain gets to the last interview: "What do you do?" "Nothing, really," the man replies. "Okay, then," says the captain, "you're in charge."

"**W**hat do you do?"

"Nothing, really."

"Okay, then, you're in charge."

This parable more or less sums up American Management Theory. Here in the land of the free and the home of the brave, we find brilliant, educated, skilled, dedicated craftsmen, laborers, technicians, and professionals from all walks of life producing on a daily basis an array of goods and services of such high quality and diversity it truly boggles the mind. The only problem is they're managed by a bunch of dorks. Somehow, during all our advancement in the arts, sciences, technology, law, and agriculture, management got left behind.

Gandhi They're Not

Most managers function more like the warden of a prison than the spiritual leader of the people.

Most American managers do not understand what the people under them actually do. As a result, most managers function more like the warden of a prison than the spiritual leader of the people. Add to this the fact that few of them have studied real management theory either seriously or at all. What they did, essentially, is give the right answer to a dying captain.

We will not attempt here to provide a remedial course for managers. There are many good texts on this subject currently gathering dust on the shelves of libraries and bookstores throughout the country. Even an attempt to summarize briefly any one of these texts would require far more time and space than our format and lazy dispositions would permit.

That's Why They Call It the Golden Rule

Instead, think back to your own experiences as an underling. Being called onto the carpet for some arbitrary shortcoming or misunderstanding may have motivated you to better performance in the short run, but in the long run it merely reinforced the darker side of your laziness and prompted you to seek out new, perhaps devious ways to stick it to your company—after all, it has stuck it to you. In contrast, think back on what it was like when, by some fluke of nature precipitated by a total eclipse of the sun, your supervisor complimented you. "Nice job. You do excellent work. You really made my day. *Thank you.* I don't know what we'd do without you." How did you feel? You felt worthy, special, appreciated. You felt great. Most important, you felt grate*ful.* At that moment, and perhaps for a few hours later, you wanted to go the extra mile for your boss. Just think how the *non-lazy* must react to such stimuli.

Unfortunately, to most managers this phenomenon is either an unknown entity or, like the pleasures of suckling, has long been forgotten. If, however, you find yourself in the enviable position of "manager"—that is, people are being paid to do your work for you—don't forget the golden rule of kindness.

Classic Management Bookshelf

Kindness is free and will make you look like a managerial genius. We're all basically castaways looking for a home. Moreover, consider the lazy *you* in your absolute most dissatisfied state of mind. Now . . . how would you like to manage *ten* such people?

Don't Rest on Your
Laurels—Sleep on Them

You: Visionary

Because your mind is not cluttered with useless facts and figures like everyone else's, you may from time to time actually accomplish something significant for your company. This will be achieved not by banging your head against the wall, but by avoiding unnecessary work and letting good ideas come to *you*. And come they will, in their own good time—but not if you're thrashing about like a dying fish. These ideas are like little angels parachuting to earth, looking for a safe place to land. Your job is to provide that place. Remember, the ideal lazy person is virtually indistinguishable from a Zen master.

Perhaps, motivated by your laziness, you can demonstrate that your company's accounting procedures are largely redundant. Or you've come up with an innovative way to farm out work to consultants, enabling your company to eliminate five positions (hopefully not yours). Or because you gave some guy at the racetrack a good tip, you're poised to win an important new account for your

> The ideal lazy person is virtually indistinguishable from a Zen master.

firm. With these ideas and opportunities knocking at your door, what do you do? Since you are trying to lay low, your effort should take the form of a suggestion at the least or a modest proposal at the most. Stay away from the messy details of implementation. Keep one foot dangling off the bandwagon at all times and jump clear off at any real sign of backfire.

You: Visionary

You: Media Star?

What you really want to do now is promote. Use every effective means available to spread word of your idea throughout the company. Promotion is as American as apple pie, so don't be hesitant to engage in it. Look at Hollywood. A studio may spend $25 million making a picture, but another $50 million promoting it. The movie isn't any good to them if no one sees it. Similarly, your idea, even once successfully implemented, is of little value to you personally if not synonymous with your name.

How do you promote your idea to your co-workers and supervisors without sounding obnoxious? How do you pat yourself on the back around the clock without wearing a hole through your

> **H**ow do you pat yourself on the back around the clock without wearing a hole through your shirt?

shirt? Unlike Hollywood, you can't plaster the walls with colorful posters that announce:

"Coming soon, to an office near you: Simplified accounting procedures by Sue Nichols of marketing! A force that could not be stopped—it came, it saw, it loaded itself onto the hard drive! 'I laughed, I cried, I cut my database in half.' "

You: Yenta

How, then, do you promote while laying low? Simple. You're already spending at least an hour or two each day making the rounds to schmooze at various cubicles and offices. Use that time for subtle promotion, dropping a few lines with each person concerning your brainchild. Make distinctions with regard to whom you're speaking. If it's someone who would benefit directly from the change, point it out in a nice way: "Hey, Don, I can help you cut down on some of the busywork you do around here. . . . I know you've got better things to do." If it's someone who perhaps will suffer from the change, take that person's side: "Jesse, this just goes to show you how upper-level management can take a perfectly good, well-intentioned idea and screw it up completely. . . ." If it's someone who will remain essentially unaffected by the change, consider whom they hang out with and adjust your statements accordingly.

What about the big honchos in upper-level management with whom you have virtually no contact, casual or otherwise? If the idea seems to be meeting with favorable reaction, make sure they know it's yours by sending a short note. Perhaps suggest small refinements in your original idea and offer to meet for such a purpose. Be sure to lavish praise on this honcho for her wise and far-thinking openness to positive change. Even if nothing results directly from this note, you can be sure you've made a friend and advanced yourself in the process.

GETTING AWAY ...
With All Sorts of Stuff

The Art of Calling
In Sick

Sick of It All

Most companies and government agencies have a strange policy. Vacation days are yours for keeps. If you don't use them during the term of your employment, you're paid for them when you leave. Sick days, on the other hand, are fleeting. If you don't use them, they tend to disappear at the end of some preestablished period. In other words, your company is telling you to avoid vacations and get sick. The least you can do is oblige—except, of course, for the part about avoiding vacations.

Getting "Real" Sick

Even though you will rarely be sick when you use a sick day, it is important to simulate a genuine episode of illness. On such a day, you would most likely wake up on the late side feeling terrible and sounding terrible. You would proceed to make the call as close as reasonably possible to starting time. A *fake* episode should transpire no differently. If you feel one of those days coming on, a moment of preparation the night before will be helpful. Even though you will be going right back to bed in the morning, set your alarm clock for a few minutes after starting time, say 8:45 A.M. Make the call immediately upon waking, thereby capturing the most disoriented, gravelly sounding you. (This can be done from other people's homes or even other time zones if necessary.)

Ill Advice

Do not, repeat, *do not* call your supervisor. He or she will be prepared with key penetrating questions to which you may not have prepared the correct replies. Instead, pick out the most sympathetic person who reports to the same supervisor and let *that person* relay the pitiful, gory details of your malady to your hard-nosed boss. Your supervisor will be reluctant to probe the situation any further for fear of being pegged as the tyrant that he is. His immediate emotional reaction of utter disbelief will be tempered by the concern of the doting grandmother type delivering the news.

Another way to avoid speaking directly to your boss is to call in sick overnight on his voice mail. Background noises can lend authenticity here. The simple sound of a toilet flushing or a medicine cabinet closing can make your boss kind of glad he won't be seeing you for a while. As a clincher, throw in a line about struggling to do some work at home—preferably a task that can't easily be verified.

Background noises can lend authenticity here.

Should you happen to speak directly to your boss on the phone, it is important to convey extreme frustration at not being able to waste another day of your life toiling robotically for company goals that mean nothing to you. In fact, hold out the possibility that you will be in later in the day, thereby planting in your boss's brain the pathetic image of a lone worker stumbling through the streets at midday, spewing phlegm, and thinking only of his tiny contribution to the Gross National Product. He may recommend you take an extra day.

Your Boss's
Vacation = Your Vacation

Send Me a Postcard

If you're lucky, you'll get two, maybe three weeks of vacation a year. If your boss is lucky, she'll get three, maybe four. Which leads us to an obvious but important point—*never* take vacation at the same time as your boss. Your boss's vacation equals your vacation anyway. Together, the two of you can combine for a five- to seven-week vacation from each other, part of which you will just happen to spend at the office.

Normally, you put a reasonable amount of planning into your out-of-the-office vacation; except for not needing a travel agent, why should your "in-house" vacation be any different? So stock that mini-fridge with Zima. Bring in that

> **G**o on "hikes" to various fun parts of the office.

tanning lamp. Go on "hikes" to various fun parts of the office or beyond the confines of the building entirely. And by all means, forward your calls to someone who *isn't* on in-house vacation.

Then *Act* Like an Adult

Hopefully, when your boss left, you and your co-workers were ROR—released on your own recognizance. If you were, there is precious little to worry about; proceed with in-house vacation. If your boss left you with a specific assignment during this time, perhaps take one or two hours a day, or even one full day out of your in-house vacation, to do as much of it as you can.

Your Boss's Vacation = Your Vacation

Because your boss will return with some combination of serenity and guilt, this minimal effort will be appreciated more than usual.

He'll Need a Vacation Soon, Too

If, however, when your boss left she designated an interim replacement or watchdog, things may be considerably more difficult. You may not be able to take the same degree of liberty. Some of your in-house vacation plans may have to be curtailed—like the luau in the small conference room. You may also have to exert effort learning your interim boss's traits and patterns—a generally inefficient expenditure of energy, particularly for the lazy person.

Worse yet, your erstwhile boss may be chock-full of distasteful ideas ranging from frequent "bed checks," to "interim progress reports," to "new initiatives." However, do not give in and surrender your well-deserved in-house vacation, regardless of your temporary boss's delusions of grandeur. At this time, it is important for you to think back to second grade and the hapless substitute teacher. No matter what his highfalutin notions of teaching

Shakespeare to seven-year-olds or warnings that "every day counts," there was no stopping the spitballs and airplanes from flying. After all, he was just the substitute—you knew it, he knew it, God knew it. The same principle will work today, in adulthood, when you deal with the interim boss.

Tapping the Reserve

Also, recall that you have several extra assignments "warehoused." Now would be a good time to tap that supply, proving to your real boss upon her return that you indeed possess the initiative she suspected you did. Any tales of woe from the interim boss will fall flat in the face of this tactic. The proof is in the pudding, and if creating a resortlike atmosphere was what it took to get this done in her absence, so be it.

Like a Second Condom

Finally, it is useful to reassure yourself that any negative reports from the interim boss will be tempered by his own sense of inadequacy. When he goes to *his* supervisor (same as yours) and tells her that people goofed off under his charge, he is effectively saying: "I am a screwup. I cannot hold down the fort." *Few* people will be so honest. Therein lies perhaps the ultimate level of protection for your in-house vacation.

Other Countries'
Work Habits

Sometimes it feels like there are no high-paying, relaxing jobs left in the United States. In which case you might consider working overseas, especially if you already have some foreign language skills. Here is a brief summary of a few overseas places.

Japan: Stay away. The work ethic in Japan has evolved into a truly pathological state. Fourteen-hour workdays and two-hour commutes are the norm. In Japan, your work is your life. Even the skimpy vacations afforded to its citizens are often spoiled by having to spend them with co-workers. Worse still, there is supposed to be some sort of "honor" in simply not taking vacations, even if they are available.

Other Places in the Pacific Rim: Bad and getting worse. Most of the economies in Asia model themselves after Japan. Did you ever stop to wonder why you can now buy a decent pair of leather sneakers for $19.95? Best to avoid working in the Pacific Rim entirely.

Western Europe: Worth considering. Europeans have a more "civilized" approach to work. Six weeks of vacation per year is fairly standard, along with a strict nine-to-five mentality and loads of holidays. Countries like Italy and France virtually shut down for the entire month of August except for tourist attractions and nightclubs. In Spain, meanwhile, siestas institutionalize on a daily basis the very naps you would otherwise have had to sneak in.

Eastern Europe: Worth a look. The work ethic in these countries has been dulled after a half century of communism. They have the same liberal work hours and vacations as their counterparts in Western Europe, but aren't expected to make up for it by being particularly productive during regular work hours. An entire subcontinent filled with U.S. postal workers.

Mexico/Latin America: Not bad, though getting worse. Most of these countries still have siestas. However, with the new North American Free Trade Agreement, Mexican workplaces are starting to mimic those in the United States. And with talk of this agreement being extended to include all of the Americas, this attitude may soon pervade the entire hemisphere.

Other Third- and Fourth-World Countries: Stay away. These people have to work hard just to provide for the basic human necessities. Clearly laziness is not a part of these cultures or they would have developed a whole bunch of shortcuts by now.

The Caribbean: Excellent conditions. Island nations never seem to develop much of a work ethic. Which brings us to that largest of island nations . . .

Australia: The tops. Australians are the laziest people on the face of the planet. Having even more liberal work ethic, hours, and vacation time than Europeans, Australians are keen to get the unpleasantness of work out of the way ASAP so they can get on to more important things like loafing around, traveling, and drinking beer. It would be a challenge for even an exceptionally lazy American to be labeled as such in Australia (though feel free to prove this to yourself).

To Beep
or Not to Beep

The Lock . . .

Wearing a beeper can be a double-edged sword. On one hand, it is yet another instrument of slavery. You might feel like a swan that is captured, tagged, and released as part of a high-tech study on migrating patterns. Your company's purpose in giving you the beeper, of course, is their convenience. They want access to you *all* of the time, not just some of the time. Stepping away from your desk to venture into the woods no longer necessarily means refuge. Whether you are gathering food, hibernating, or even mating, your supervisor—your very own Marlin Perkins—reserves the right at any time to signal you and await your trained response.

> **Y**ou might feel like a swan that is captured, tagged, and released as part of a high-tech study on migrating patterns.

. . . Or the Key?

On the other hand, the beeper can actually be liberating. Remember, it is only a one-way device. Unlike in the case of the migrating swan, no one actually knows *where* you are—only that wherever that may be, you can be reached. With this knowledge, therefore, you can roam freely in the world (that is, within the beeper's signaling radius) and still log paid time "at the office." Upper-level management's perennial complaint that they were looking for you but could not find you loses virtually all its validity. If it was at all important, they could have beeped you. In essence, wherever you are—the park, the zoo, a matinee—you can safely assume that if you're not hearing a beep, there's no problem.

Cover Your Beepin' Butt

Of course, when you do get beeped, it makes sense to be either near the office itself or near someplace where you have some legitimate business-related purpose. Sleeping in a locker room or library within a five-minute walking distance of the office, for instance, will easily give you enough time to scurry back and make the return phone call from your desk. Official excuse: You were in the bathroom when they beeped you. If you are significantly farther from the office, however, select in advance a location near a client's office or some other place you could conceivably visit. If it's a client's office you've selected, you'll need your whereabouts verified if and when the beep comes.

Official excuse: You were in the bathroom when they beeped you.

In such a case, show up at the client's office with a story ready and make the call. An easier remedy, however, is to walk into a nearby copy shop and make the call from there. Tell your supervisor you were pricing out a printing job. With annoying mechanical noise overheard in the background, the veracity of your story will rarely be questioned.

Saved by the Beep

Another advantage of the beeper is its use as an "out" during boring meetings. If you anticipate such a meeting—the kind that has you playing tic-tac-toe with yourself in the margins of your notepad—arrange for a friend or relative to beep you about ten minutes in. When the beep goes off, feign disappointment at the interruption. Consider even muttering an expletive under your breath. Turn on the acting charm. It's Academy Awards time. You were looking forward to this meeting and were just about to make a salient point. Apologize briefly as you skulk out the door and shake your head. Just make

Responding to the Beep

sure people feel sorry for you. An hour, a day, or a week later, tell everyone about how the gas company detected a leak in your home, or how your dog required emergency bladder surgery—that is, if anyone even brings it up.

They Even Sell Fake Ones Now

Finally, no discussion of the beeper would be complete without mention of one highly important fact: It makes you *look* important. This is especially true outside the office, where no one really knows what it is you do (or don't do). You're more likely to get swift service at a restaurant or shoe store while wearing the beeper. Whether people surmise that you're a doctor or lawyer, police detective or drug dealer, the effect is the same: respect, fear, your main course arriving just as your appetizer is finished. For similar reasons, the beeper is also useful for impressing a date. And if that date isn't going so well, it can be instrumental in *ending* that date prematurely, not unlike the boring meeting.

The "Job-Sharing Option"

Get a Life

In the nineties, more and more "hip" companies are offering the job-sharing option. Little do they know, you've already been sharing your job for years, with various unsuspecting fellow employees. The job-sharing option referred to here, however, is a more formal version. The idea goes something like this: Two people each work half-time to do what was formerly one person's full-time job—yours, perhaps.

If this opportunity presents itself to you and you can afford it (we've heard they cut *pay* in half, too), take it. Here's one way to look at the bounty this option represents. If your company gives you two weeks of vacation per year, you will enjoy only fifty vacation weeks *total* by the time you retire in, say, twenty-five years. Can a few trips to EuroDisney and Atlantic City truly compensate you for a lifetime of noble, painstaking service to the Corporate Gods? However, with the job-sharing option, half of every week is a vacation. You can collect a lifetime's worth of vacation in only two years. In ten years, you can collect *five* lifetime's worth.

One Born Every Minute

Of utmost importance is with *whom* you share your job. If you have any control over this aspect, make sure it is someone far less lazy than yourself. In the best-case scenario, this will be someone newly hired trying to work his way into the company full-time. He will need someone to show him the ropes—you know, those same ropes that have conveniently slipped through your hands so many key times without leaving even a minor burn. You will play the role of trainer, teacher, gym teacher (remember *those* ropes?), whatever. As long as he recognizes his golden opportunity to learn from a pro.

You two will make a wonderful tag team, you leaving assignments, he doing them. Like Caine's teacher on the old *Kung Fu* program, you will dispense your bits of wisdom in obscure, impenetrable twenty-second nuggets he will have to spend the rest of the show (the week?) figuring out. "How do you print something out in WordPerfect?" he asks. Don't even *think* of telling him: "Shift-F7." Instead, you should respond: "What is the sound of one hand typing?" Each day will bring with it a new koan. Not until he can answer all his koans and snatch a paper clip from your hand has he attained complete knowledge. Just like doing your work, these are part of his "dues." Of course, nothing good lasts forever. If you sense your partner is about to graduate to taking all of what was once your nine-to-five job, make a preemptive strike— get out.

Just Like the Sixties, Man

If you are lucky, your next job-sharing assignment will be with someone like you—a lazy person. After your harrowing experience with the go-getter,

The Job-Sharing Option

you'll be better able to appreciate the comfort and security of settling down with a kindred spirit. As soon as the two of you realize you were cut from the same mold, you can get started doing together perhaps even less work than you once did alone.

A problem, however, may arise. Unfortunately, *some* output must still come from this less-than-dynamic duo. Just like championship football or basketball teams where good players feed off of each other's energy to achieve more together than they ever could have separately, you and your like-minded job-sharing partner might feed off of each other's laziness to the point where absolutely zero work gets done, putting you both in jeopardy. While this state of affairs is enviable, it is unfortunately doomed to failure. To break the stalemate, we recommend a friendly flip of the coin from time to time. With a little cooperation, the two of you can prove to the world that sometimes the whole can be less than the sum of the parts.

Or Call Dr. Kevorkian

There is one more job-share possibility we haven't yet mentioned. That possibility is a worst-case scenario and is so horrible we shudder even to think about it. You may get stuck with someone who is average or somewhat above average in her productivity, understands the work, and is wise to both your identity and your tricks. She has no intention of putting up with your schemes and being taken advantage of, nor is she willing to take the easy route by lowering her own productivity. You have a problem on your hands. In this case, there is little choice: You must ask for a reassignment or transfer due to "incompatibility" as soon as you have recognized the predicament. Don't worry about what upper-level management might think or about possibly hurting your erstwhile partner's feelings; she has probably already put in for a transfer herself.

Lazy Parenting: Hiding Behind Your Kids

Think Back to Your Last Plane Trip

The lazy parent: A contradiction in terms? An oxymoron? Maybe. Ironically, becoming a parent can be the consequence of one of the laziest (and most enjoyable) moments in your life. Perhaps just as ironically, it can also be the result of years of careful planning, tens of thousands of dollars in fertility procedures, and months of making love with a thermometer in one hand and a calendar in the other.

Either way, the result is the same—roughly two decades (these days more like three) of hard work, immeasurable responsibility, and nervousness that sits in your stomach like a decomposing car battery. Ultimately, having kids is a deeply personal decision—or oversight. If you don't have any kids yet, take a good, long look at the weary, cranky, puffy-eyed folks who drag themselves through the office door every morning muttering garbled phrases about how the knobs and buttons on the stereo are missing.

> **W**hat if you already have kids? There's good news. You can keep them.

Ask About Our Free Checking

But what if you already have kids? Well, there's good news. You can keep them. Not only that, you can hide behind them. Since before recorded time, parents have contended, boasted, and lamented that they are "protecting" their children. Nonsense. In fact, it's been the other way around. Kids have been protecting their *parents*—from doing things they don't like to do and from seeing themselves as they'd prefer not to. Having kids can provide perhaps the broadest array of excuses with which to shuck off society's expectations and not only get away with it, but be applauded and adulated for it as well. Now that you're a parent, welcome to the cushiest club never discussed in public—someone had to let the cat out of the bag. As a lazy person, you should inquire freely about the privileges of membership.

"But I Have a Note!"

For starters, there are the basic excuses for everything under the sun. Unable to hand in a report on time? Your infant son took a wee-wee on it. Arrive late to work? Your kid woke up screaming in the middle of the night. Like a good parent, you sat up with her and told her a story

Unable to hand in a report on time? Your infant son took a wee-wee on it.

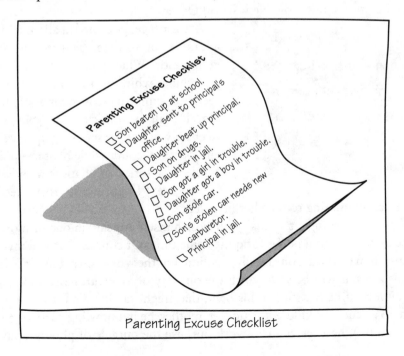

Parenting Excuse Checklist

till she fell back asleep. Feel like leaving work early? Your son has to be picked up from kindergarten. Get the sudden urge to leave in the middle of the day? Your child has some sort of problem at school. State or imply something that will engender sympathy, such as your daughter was being picked on by the other kids because she put on mismatched socks. Feel like not coming in to work at all today? No problem—your seven-year-old daughter conveniently woke up with the flu, and you have to stay home to take care of her.

Photo Opportunity

Whether or not any of these things actually occurred is of little importance. What counts is whether the stories are believable. So make them *sound* believable. If you're a man, take particular advantage of these excuses and their variations. As we near the end of the century, people from all walks of life are finding themselves overwhelmed by a flood of guilt and a torrent of "family values." Nothing fits in better with this mind-set than the thought of a man revealing his feminine side by becoming overly involved with his children. Learn to exploit the New World Order.

> When you smell danger approaching, whip out the photos and use them not unlike a cross to fend off Dracula.

At the office, be armed at all times with adorable up-to-date pictures of your young kids. When you smell danger approaching, whip out the photos and use them not unlike a cross to fend off Dracula. It will be difficult for your boss to chew you out for screwing up a bread-and-butter account while he stares point-blank at a series of snapshots showing your cute, bright-eyed, rosy-cheeked daughter attempting to take her first steps.

If you can arrange it so that your boss himself appears in one or more of these pictures, you'll be set for quite some time. Of course, that will involve inviting him to at least one family function, but the work you avoid in the long run as a result will be well worth the one day of awkwardness, dread, and discomfort. If he has kids of his own, that might facilitate an invitation for them to attend one kiddie function or another, be it a bowling party or a trip to the zoo. Whatever you can work out, use the miracle of photography to your advantage. One word of caution, however. Make sure that Barney does not turn up in *any* of these photos, or they will surely backfire. While people will tend to adore your kids, they are sick as hell of fat, purple dinosaurs.

Sacrificing the Firstborn

To avert a major work crisis, when mere photos simply won't cut it, try bringing your child in to work. Never underestimate the power of a live appearance. Compare, as a child yourself once, the impact of bringing in to school a baseball card of a given player to the impact of bringing in that player himself—there *is* no comparison. Pull no punches. On D-Day, march Junior right into the office of whichever supervisory figure is attempting to ruin your life. His negative thoughts regarding the slug that he sees you to be and the pain-filled special assignment he's aching to give you will be no match for your genuine, own-flesh-and-blood protective suit of armor.

> On D-Day, march Junior right into the office of whichever supervisory figure is attempting to ruin your life.

This is where weeks of rehearsal will finally pay off. Now is the time for that nursery rhyme or adorably sung kiddie song. Whether for the moment she's London Bridge falling down or a little teapot short and stout, make sure she breaks hearts—your boss's in particular. A song that incorporates your boss's name—in a positive way, of course—is a big plus. A clever little dance number won't hurt, either. There shouldn't be a dry eye left in the room. For extra insurance, have your daughter give your boss a peck on the cheek, no matter how much it may disgust her or you. Don't just win, baby—win big. And on the way out, pay a quick visit with your child to everyone else, if only for good measure.

Review Old Episodes of *The Brady Bunch*

As they get older and certain opportunities to hide behind your children fade away, other opportunities will take their place. Children in the early part of grade school frequently experience adjustment problems, leading to refusals to go to school, abstinence from food other than sugar-coated junk, and even attempts to "run away" from home. These crises—whether they occur or not—all may serve as entirely appropriate excuses for your less-than-sterling performance at work. Likewise, in the latter part of grade school, fights among kids—be they simply name-calling or well-equipped gang fights over "territory"—are common. Take full advantage.

Rebel with a Cause

> These years will provide virtually unlimited opportunity for Mommy and Daddy's truancy.

Adolescence, of course, brings with it unprecedented trauma, both for the child and for you. Whether it's your daughter dating her first biker or your son experiencing his first "flashback," these years will provide virtually unlimited opportunity for Mommy and Daddy's truancy. And finally, there is college. Around this time, unfortunately, the well of child-related excuses will have run almost dry, with Junior leaving home to make his way. Not to worry, though. The well can be replenished by your poverty-driven request for a fat raise, which you will most likely get. College—whether or not your child actually attends—can in this way prove to be a valuable investment in the future.

The Joy of Imaginary Parenthood

"But I Played One on TV"

So far, all these suggestions have assumed you really had at least one child. This assumption, however, should not be taken as absolute. While actually having children is sufficient for applying these techniques, it is not necessary. With a little creativity, childless couples (or even childless singles) can employ them as well. It is often said that nothing is more rewarding yet *less* demanding than faking parenthood.

> **N**othing is more rewarding yet *less* demanding than faking parenthood.

Faking parenthood can essentially be divided into two phases: faking pregnancy and faking the rest. A male employee will certainly have an easier time of faking the pregnancy than will his female counterpart. The male employee may be able to pull it off with nothing more than an occasional tale of his wife's morning sickness. Skimming a book or two on pregnancy will add an air of authenticity to his laments.

A female employee, on the other hand, has it much harder. She must actively fake the pregnancy, day in, day out. This means both realistically and progressively stuffing clothing, feigning morning sickness, visibly eating bizarre foods in even more bizarre proportions, using makeup creatively to create the facial impression that she is carrying life, and mastering the mommy-to-be duck-walk. The lazy woman must ask herself if all this is worth it, and may want to consider faking *adoption* instead.

Faking the rest isn't terribly difficult, whether you are a phony mom *or* an apocryphal dad. You can use essentially the same excuses discussed in the previous chapter. Those excuses will serve both to lessen your workload *and* to reinforce the existence of your nonexistent child. Borrowing a friend's or relative's child, perhaps in exchange for good tickets to a ball game, may suffice when displaying photos or bringing the child to the office. As in faking a pregnancy, skimming a book or two on child rearing will be of great use.

A Note on the Refrigerator Will Help

However, a word of caution is necessary. As time goes by and you have occasion to embellish the life of your nonexistent child, make sure your stories are consistent. Keep track of what you're saying. Take notes if necessary. Otherwise, people at the office may wonder why Ronny is now called Ricky. Or why your son started out with jet-black hair and wound up a redhead. Or why your daughter has been "two" for five years running. Fake parents have been known to make the most fundamental errors when they don't pay attention. As insurance, consider writing a bio on your fake child and using it to quiz yourself from time to time. For instance, is your child a boy or a girl?

> Take notes if necessary. Otherwise, people at the office may wonder why Ronny is now called Ricky.

As a matter of fact, it is important to cover yourself whether you are a real *or* fake parent. For instance, if you claim you're spending the day at home with your (real) sick daughter, make sure your boss doesn't have a (real) son in the same school who not only saw her in class the same day but tried to slip an eraser down her shirt. Or if you bring your young (impostor) son to the company picnic, make sure the CEO's daughter doesn't associate him with a different family in town and start ugly rumors of kidnapping. The bottom line here is this: When hiding behind your kids, do at least as good a job as *they* would at hiding behind *you*.

Jury Duty

Twelve Lazy Men

Every citizen of the United States, when accused of a crime, has the constitutional right to be judged by a group of his or her peers in a court of law. By serving on a jury, you are not only helping to promote justice in the short run, but you are also becoming a link in the long chain of liberty that extends from way back in colonial times up to today and beyond. More importantly, you're getting out of work for a few days.

  Check if your company or agency pays you for time served on a jury. If it does, you will probably want to get out of the office for a while and try something different. Listening to the gory details of a drug-related drive-by shooting while you catch up on crossword puzzles might just be that something. On the other hand, this, too, may grow tiresome. Study and master the methods that will allow *you* to determine the length of your time as a juror, whether it's one day or several months.

  First, you may not want to serve at all, either because your company does not pay for your time or because you already have better work avoidance plans for the next couple of weeks. Be aware that, on a jury, strolling into the courtroom two or three hours after the morning session of the trial has begun is frowned upon, even *with* a note from your doctor. And sitting

Sitting relatively still for four hours a day without the aid of Sega Genesis may not be your cup of tea.

relatively still for hours a day without the aid of Sega Genesis may not be your cup of tea. In any case, if you're picked for jury duty and want to get right out of it, here are some things you can say or do.

Five Things to Say or Do to Get Out of Jury Duty Right Away

1. "What are my chances of a book deal on this case?"
2. "I don't want to say I've made up my mind already, but the defendant's tarot card reading was not so hot."
3. "Your honor, I will provide the same impartiality I received when *I* was on trial for armed robbery."
4. "Do we get out of work for the execution, too?"
5. "What if my affair with the defendant was only a very brief and meaningless one?"

If you become progressively bored with the trial or decide for any reason that your urge to laziness would be better satisfied elsewhere, here are some things you can blurt out during the trial.

Five Things to Blurt Out During the Trial to Relieve You of Jury Duty

1. "Look, Geraldo says he's innocent . . . so he's innocent."
2. "Can I be sequestered with the *cute* jurors?"
3. (while chugging from a bottle of Jack Daniel's): "Circumstantial, shmurcumstantial—fellas, let's get this show on the road!"
4. (to the defendant): "I swore I'd get you, you bastard!"
5. (to the defendant): "Wait a second, *that's* where I know you from. I was your 'bitch' in prison."

If, however, you are sure being a juror suits your schedule, go down to your county courthouse and make certain you're on the appropriate list. Once your name comes up, you'll want to say all the *right* things to be selected.

Five Things to Say to Be Selected for the Jury

1. "Hi. I just got back from a thirty-six-month human isolation experiment in Antarctica. . . . What's up?"

2. "O.J. *who*?"
3. "I had an opinion once, but it died of loneliness."
4. "Well, maybe he had a perfectly good *reason* to open fire in a crowded pavilion."
5. "Where *am* I?"

As we said, do what you like during the trial itself, as long as it's not too conspicuous. Books, a Walkman, stationery for letters to old friends are all appropriate. Don't become obsessed with consuming every little detail of the case. There are eleven other jurors. *One* of them will know what went on.

Once you are sequestered to reach a decision, you may soon find you have had enough and want to be dismissed. In such a case, be a chameleon—go with the flow and speed up the verdict. Or exhibit signs of a nervous breakdown. Or pick a fistfight. Or start an affair with another juror (hotel room already paid for). Or take it upon yourself to hold a press conference.

> **T**here are eleven other jurors. *One* of them will know what went on.

If, however, you like the way you're killing time and you'd like the process to go on indefinitely, the procedure is a bit trickier. You must be the counterweight that continually steers the group toward being a hung jury. Change directions like an Olympic skier. Swim against the tide. Keep your peers from reaching the "easy" verdict—that is, any verdict at all.

Five Things to Say to Prevent or Delay a Verdict

1. "How do *you* know? Did you *see* her kill him?"
2. "Forget about the alibi. The guilt is written all over his face."
3. "But what you're saying, in effect, is that there still *is* that one-in-a-billion chance that two people have the exact same DNA."
4. "Sure he confessed. But did he say it with *feeling*?"
5. "Since when is taking care of the *family business* a crime?"

Before a mistrial has finally been declared, you may have racked up several fun-filled weeks or even months of paid "vacation." Before returning to work,

Prolonging Jury Duty

be sure to put in for a few sick days. Surely your company has heard of post-trial stress disorder.

Pick Me, Monty

Finally, what if you'd like to go on jury duty but months or years have gone by and you haven't been called? Go down to your county clerk's office (during work hours, if possible) and make sure you're on the appropriate list. If after this you're still not called, no problem. Just tell your boss you *have* been called. Only the most paranoid employer will bother to check this out. Most likely, you can take off right then for a couple of weeks. The night before you decide to come back to work, rent or go see a good movie with a trial in it—*Twelve Angry Men, A Few Good Men, The Verdict*—or just watch Court TV for a few minutes. Like the folks who really are on trial, you might need a good alibi.

> **L**ike the folks who really are on trial, you might need a good alibi.

The Family and
Medical Leave Act

Friends of Bill

Whatever the judgment of journalists, historians, and the general public eventually holds for Bill Clinton, the lazy will forever point to his administration as an unqualified success for its first day alone. On that day, January 21, 1993, Bill Clinton signed into law the Family and Medical Care Leave Act (FMLA). This law entitles most employees to a total of twelve weeks' unpaid leave (with medical benefits) during any twelve-month period—to care for a newborn child, newly adopted child, or child newly received in foster care, within the first twelve months of the child's birth, adoption, or arrival; or to care for a seriously ill spouse, child under eighteen, or disabled adult, child, or parent; or to receive medical care for one's own serious health condition.

In some circumstances, this may include leave to care for an ill relative or domestic partner. In most cases, an employee who returns from FMLA leave is guaranteed to be restored to the same or equivalent position he or she left.

Thank you, Bill. Thank you, Senate. Thank you, House. In addition to those people who actually need such a leave, there are millions more of us who just feel

> In addition to those people who actually need such a leave, there are millions more of us who just feel like taking it.

like taking it. Most of us can find a way to skip a few paychecks each year as long as we know we're coming back and our medical benefits are maintained (in case we really *do* get sick). Face it: Physically coming in to work—

commuting, buying lunch, chipping in for birthday and going-away presents—often approaches half our salary anyway. Live cheaply at home or spend your leave "visiting" a long-lost friend and you're there, dude.

Or Dabble with Plastic Surgery

And no matter what you do with your leave, you can be certain of one thing: It will blow away the measly two- or three-week "paid" vacation you normally get. What can you do in a couple of weeks? Fly to some expensive place, unpack, drop a wheelbarrow full of currency, repack, fly home, and start the next fifty-week countdown. Three months, on the other hand, is enough time to get back into that wonderful rhythm of getting up late and hanging out; enough time to catch up on years worth of movies you had been meaning to see; enough time to find a new love, ride a long and interesting emotional roller coaster, and finally break it off; in essence, enough time to forget that you ever *had* a job. And when you *do* eventually come back to work (to pay the video rental charges), your next lengthy leave of absence will be only thirty-nine weeks away. Even this period will be broken up nicely by the two-week paid vacation to which you are still entitled.

"My Pet Ferret Has the Blahs"

Unless you have been living in a bubble for the past two decades, you undoubtedly are suffering from some minor medical syndrome.

Convincing your place of work that you qualify for this leave of absence shouldn't be difficult. Unless you were dropped off in the middle of a prairie by an alien spaceship, chances are you have a relative or a "close friend" somewhere who isn't feeling too great and can prove it with a doctor's note. Officially you will be shacking up with that person for the next twelve weeks, even if unofficially you are somewhere in Mexico, drinking tequila and "finding yourself."

By the same token, unless you have been living inside a bubble for the past two decades, you undoubtedly are suffering from some minor medical syndrome that can be overindulged by a willing physician covered by your health package. If not, go to a chiropractor—he will tell you your whole skeletal structure is out of whack and that you will be requiring months worth of "adjustments." Or go to a professional psychoanalyst—she will tell you either that your rage is masking your depression or that your depression is masking your rage (choose one, please). Either way, you will be needing years of therapy.

Have a Nice Life

It is worth noting that some state and local laws provide leave opportunities that are even more expansive than federal law. In New York City, for instance, an unpaid child care leave of absence shall be granted to an employee who becomes the parent of a child up to four years of age, either by birth or adoption, or whose registered domestic partner becomes the parent of a child up to four years of age, either by birth or adoption, or whose registered domestic partner becomes the parent of a child up to four years of age, for a period of *up to forty-eight months*. Proving you're a new parent (see "The Joy of Imaginary Parenthood") is a bit more difficult than proving you're merely sick (see "The Art of Calling In Sick"), but possible nonetheless.

You can start a whole other career during this time, complete with an extra educational degree and on-the-job training. You may tire of this job, too, and take an extended leave of absence from it as well. You can even repeat this process several times, eventually finding yourself on a leave within a leave within a leave. This is no doubt an enviable position. With the wisdom that time, experience, and comparison bring, you will have your pick of a variety of jobs to return to.

> You can start a whole other career during this time, complete with an extra educational degree and on-the-job training.

The Family and Medical Leave Act

"Have You Seen Our New Copier?"

What happens on your job while you are gone? Nothing that didn't happen while you were there.

By the way, what happens at your job while you are gone? Nothing that didn't happen while you were there. Supervisors look for scapegoats. Employees run for cover. Your work is now done by someone else. Or by no one else. Truly, it does not matter.

If and when you do return to a given job, you will be surprised at how little has changed. For instance, you may think the four years you have missed is a long time. After all, a third of all marriages don't last that long. Babies are conceived, gestated, delivered, potty-trained, and sent to preschool in this time. Presidential administrations rise and fall. Sports "dynasties" come and go. Entire continents realign themselves politically and economically. Nonetheless, your stack of folders will likely be right where you left it. So will that horrendous stain on the carpet. And two of the four secretaries in your group will still be there, typing away, eating what seems like the *exact same sandwich* they were working on when you last laid eyes on them. Basically, everything will be roughly as you left it. Unless, of course, in the interim your company has folded.

GETTING OUT

And Now the End Is Near . . .

When to Bother Switching Jobs

By this point, having mastered most of the methods in this book, we hope that you have created a lazy-person's utopia for yourself. Unfortunately, though, no utopia lasts forever. Sometimes forces beyond your control change the climate for the worse and rather permanently. Obviously, starting from scratch and having to rebuild the temple is a frightening thought. But sometimes it's the only way. Before you take this drastic step, make sure at least two of the following seven signs are present.

1. **A new boss comes on the scene who's out to prove himself.** You know you're in trouble if he starts displaying any of the following characteristics: bed checks, artificial deadlines, productivity harangues, or suggesting that you work weekends. If he was hired by his dad or uncle, you are mincemeat. He will continually try to demonstrate that he "deserves" his job— that those rumors of nepotism are false. Though they're true, of course, he will run you into the ground trying to prove otherwise.

2. **You start becoming so bored with the job that you can't even maintain your four hours (or even two hours) of productive output per day.** You may reach the point where attempting to sell one more set of storm windows to one more general contractor will put you on suicide watch. Time to get out. Though you can be plenty lazy when you're dead, you can't really enjoy it the same way.

3. **Your secluded office is switched to a high-visibility one.** With nothing else to do, folks at the top often commission "studies." If the latest study

indicates that moving your office away from the sandwich machine and nearer to the boss will get you more "involved," it's time to get uninvolved—permanently.

4. **You start getting "high-visibility" assignments.** What if it's your call—do we get by with our old steel mill or do we invest a billion dollars upgrading? By the time you have an answer ready, you should be working somewhere else.

5. **Layoffs are announced.** Even if you survive the cut, your workload will escalate. You may even be subject to that old ploy of "added responsibility in lieu of a raise." The phrase lean and *mean* is no accident. This kind of meanness usually sends company stocks soaring. It should send you out the door. Before you leave, buy some company stock.

6. **They make you punch a clock.** A new policy of signing in and signing out may be implemented or an existing one may suddenly be enforced. This is particularly grim when coupled with "redlining": drawing of a redline by management in the sign-in book after the official cutoff time for morning arrivals, say at 9:05. Some combination of verbal warnings, paycheck deductions, and disciplinary action will usually follow. This policy shift is among the bleakest because it reinforces on a daily basis the very fear that we try our best to dismiss—the fear that our company owns us. Few feelings are more degrading than running down the hall at 9:04 as those who have already "made it" look on in amusement. Since that strategy never works in the long run to enhance productivity, it is usually a sure sign that the company has fallen on hard times and is headed for more of the same.

   If the sign-ins and redlining are strictly enforced and permanent, you ought to look into signing out for the last time.

7. **Your cover is blown.** If you are no longer allowed to work as part of (that is, hide behind) a team, if you suddenly notice a video surveillance camera in the bathroom stalls where you like to nap, or if you observe someone in a trench coat following you during one of those three-hour lunches, you know your company has your number. In this case you need to get the number of a good head hunter.

The Lazy Person's
Letter of Resignation
Do-It-Yourself Kit

For whatever reason, you're ready to move on. Your recent job search efforts have paid off handsomely. Perhaps you've been offered a job with greater pay, fewer hours, or both. Maybe at your new job they'll let you "work" at home on Mondays and Fridays. Perhaps it's one of those jobs where you're mostly "out in the field," and you "check in" only once a week or so. Or maybe your rich uncle has died and left you a hefty sum, removing you entirely from the rat race.

In any case, you're leaving and you're glad. But there's so much to do in your final few days: having the movers come to get your convertible couch, making sure the woman or the guy you had a crush on has your new number, getting back your Final Doom diskettes from your friend across the hall. The supermodels wall calendar, the back issues of *Car and Driver*, the Nerf basketball set—everything must go. The last thing you feel like doing is writing a letter of resignation. So we've done it for you. We've even written one for each of three different general situations. All you have to do is fill in the blanks.

Situation #1
You Think You Might Want to Come Back Someday

Dear *(———):*

It is with a profound sense of regret that I am resigning my position at *(company name)*, effective *(date in near future)*. When I arrived at *(company name)*, *(# years)* and *(# months)* ago, I was impressed by the dedication I saw around me and intimidated by the challenges I knew lay ahead. Today, as I reluctantly look beyond *(company name)*, I would like to believe I have absorbed some of that dedication and met some of those challenges. As a result, I have grown tremendously, not only as a *(your profession)*, but also as a *(your species)*.

While to some a job is just a job, my time here was more like a *(name of enjoyable activity, unlike job)*. I remember how overwhelmed I must have seemed the first time I *(trivial business-related activity)*. It's hard to believe that comes as second nature today. Or how about the time I *(mistake costing company less than $100)*? I felt crushed. My co-workers could justifiably have *(name of punishment, usually deadly)*, but instead they *(sickeningly sweet gesture)*. I will always remember their kindness.

But above all else, I will always remember you and the wisdom you demonstrated at the helm. What we do here isn't easy, and the problems seem to work their way up to you. Somehow, you turn them around and send them back down as solutions. Watching this process and being a small part of it is a high I had attained previously only by *(non-drug-related activity)*. However, some of life's circumstances are beyond my control, such as my *(family member)*'s unfortunate bout with *(dreaded disease)*. Therefore, I bid adieu to my greater family here while I do what I can to help *(him/her)*.

Sincerely,

(your name)

Situation #2
You Doubt You'll Ever Be Back, But It Can't Hurt to Leave the Door Open a Crack

Dear *(———)*:

It is with regret that I resign my position at *(company name)*, effective *(date in near future)*. My time at *(company name)* was a time of personal and professional growth, and for that opportunity I am grateful. Growth is achieved not in triumph alone but also in difficulty. It is the way we handled those difficulties as a team that will always stand out in my mind. It would please me if you consider me always available for advice or consultation. Unfortunately, I will be conducting research on the *(aboriginal tribe)* and living in a *(primitive-type dwelling)* somewhere in *(region not linked electronically to rest of world)* and will therefore be unreachable through normal means. However, it's the thought that counts, and mine will always be positive where *(company name)* is concerned.

Sincerely,

(your name)

Situation #3
You Are Never Coming Back

Dear *(———)*:

In case the barrage of rumors, the onslaught of bathroom graffiti, and my own recent record-breaking string of absences hasn't already somehow penetrated your thick Neanderthal skull, allow me to make it official—I am resigning; I quit, I'm outta here, sayonara, bub-bye. Where am I going? Why should *you* care? You didn't give a rat's behind about me in the *(# years)* and *(# months)* I was here, so why on earth would you start now? Caring wasn't exactly your style. Essentially, as long as you can come in, abuse your subordinates, *(incredibly embarrassing activity your boss tried to keep a secret)*, and collect a paycheck, you're happy as a pig in slop.

But alas, you owe no apologies. Rather it is the fault of a dysfunctional system that would let a miserable, bubble-headed twerp such as yourself parade proudly through life with the absurd title of *(your boss's title)*.

Sincerely,

(your name)

The Lame-Duck Syndrome

All Good Things

Your final days on the job can be your happiest and most carefree. In these final two to four weeks, your already considerably scaled down responsibilities can be reduced to a blissful nothing if you play your cards right. Although these days may be few in number, they just might turn out to be your golden days. But beware of the pitfalls.

Pop psychology tells us that those who face death, catastrophe, or dramatic change experience five phases of emotion: denial, anger, bargaining, depression, and finally acceptance. Because you're basically ecstatic to be leaving, you will probably whiz through the first four phases in a few minutes and get right to good old number five. Your co-workers, however, will not have it as easy. Remember, they're staying. Your leaving underscores that fact. Strangely enough, your departure—your liberation—is not only a death in their little family, but also a sad reminder that they are still trapped. As a result of these factors, your co-workers will tend to linger on number one, denial. You have a responsibility to see to it that they get over this hang-up, not only because you are a caring human being, but mainly because you don't need to be saddled with any more work.

Read My Lips

The key to getting your co-workers over denial is your ability to present them with the stark reality. In case gossip of your imminent departure has not spread sufficiently, spread it yourself. A note in everyone's mailbox will do, as

> **G**et past the aphorisms quickly and make it clear that you will be accepting no new work.

will E-mail. Make it short and sweet. Get past the aphorisms quickly and make it clear that you will be accepting no new work. Reinforce that policy by promptly changing the outgoing message on your voice mail. The message should state the name and phone number of the person who will be taking over what is left of your responsibilities and restate the fact that you will be accepting *no new work*.

As far as old work is concerned, there should be little problem if any. In the name of making a smooth transition for the ultimate benefit of the company, have your boss immediately establish which hangers-on will be taking over your various projects. Perhaps he'll allow you to select these people yourself—that is, if you haven't already. The truly lazy person will have selected these people—whether they knew it or not—in the very early days of his job. Only now it's official.

The Exit Interview

Odds and Ends

As your days on the payroll wane to a precious few, make yourself scarce. Use up any remaining sick days you have. When you *do* come in, time your appearance conveniently with going-away luncheons or parties being thrown in your honor. Missing your own blow-out bashes may be construed as insensitive. Besides, you might get some neat presents.

When you do come in, make good use of your time. Drop by the personnel office at least once to make sure your last paycheck or two are headed to the correct mailing address and that they include any unused vacation pay or other benefits you've accrued. Bring in a bunch of empty cardboard boxes and leave them strewn about your desk for days on end. Along with a few piles of folders pulled out and scattered around the area, they will give the impression of someone working hard on his way up and out, even though your real packing will be done in about thirty minutes sometime during your very last day.

You will almost certainly be asked to participate in an exit interview. It's odd that even though everyone knows or thinks he knows why you're leaving, this charade is nonetheless a requirement. Apparently, modern companies like to accumulate data on their own short-

> **D**on't worry about failing the exit interview. You will still be allowed to exit.

comings. Smile and give them what they want. And don't worry about failing the exit interview. You will still be allowed to exit.

Retirement—How to Know It's Begun

You are no longer in a tiny room with four walls, a window, and a three-by-five-inch framed photograph of the life partner who has kept you afloat for decades. There is no message on your voice mail threatening your dismissal for sheer incompetence. Gone is the Gameboy you kept in the small right-hand drawer of your desk. Nowhere to be found is the special seat cushion left over from the days immediately following hemorrhoid surgery. Absent is the daily planner, with pages as blank as the day you bought it. These are all signs that you've retired. It may be hard to discern at first. The warm, sunny beaches; the cool drinks with little umbrellas stuck in them; the gentle hum of the golf cart motor. These are all clues.

Hopefully, you've acquired your freedom sooner rather than later, through a good retirement plan, an inheritance, or your state lottery. Whatever the case, whether you are in your twenties or your sixties, it is a welcomed event. And because you have been quietly preparing for this moment all your life, your transition will be smooth, even seamless.

> Because you have been quietly preparing for this moment all your life, your transition will be smooth, even seamless.

Depending upon how you look at it, your life's work is either over—or perhaps has just begun. No, we don't mean more phoning, faxing, and filing. We mean helping other lazy people who maybe don't have it as good. Take them under your wing. Give them the benefit of your years and experience. Let them in on the tricks of the trade. Explain to them in great detail how you beat the system. Show them the lazy person's Ten Commandments, which follows. Better still, tell them where to buy this book.

Retirement and Beyond

The Ten Commandments
of Highly Lazy
(& Successful) People

1. **Lay Low and Don't Make the Big Mistake.** As long as you don't do something egregiously wrong, you'll win the war of attrition. Just sit back and watch the "high fliers" with their "high-exposure" projects getting shot down.
2. **Shave at least fifteen minutes off each end of the workday and add fifteen minutes on either side of lunch.** This strategy provides you with the equivalent of one *Bonanza* rerun per day in the manner least likely to arouse suspicion.
3. **Maintain four hours of productive output per day (when possible).** Just keep up this steady effort day in and day out when you can and you're liable not to ever have to break a sweat on the job. The key to this regimen is to make sure your work actually is productive output (stuff the boss will see) and not pseudo work. We recommend jump-starting your mornings, thereby allowing you to coast through the afternoon.
4. **Maintain a busy-looking office, preferably in an isolated location.** Provides camouflage and added protection from boss's bed checks.
5. **Artfully maximize your sick and vacation days.** If they give it, take it!
6. **Try to live close to work.** It sounds ironic that living close to work is something a lazy person should be concerned with, but an extra twenty minutes off your commute each way really adds up when factored over a year—equivalent to twenty extra days off a year (or all your vacation days and holidays combined)! Meanwhile, make people *think* you live far from work—fake the commute.

7. **Avoid bosses who conduct bed checks.** A boss who snoops around to ensure his "resource" is working constantly is anathema to the lazy person.

8. **Front-load your efforts.** Choose your career moves carefully so you don't inadvertently find yourself in a sweatshop. Likewise, instead of attacking new projects with "brute force," always try to determine the easiest way to get things done.

9. **Be kind to people at work.** A few kind words will do a lot more to advance your career than hours of extra drudgery in the office day in and day out.

10. **Delegate as much as possible.** This is, of course, easiest if you have a staff to delegate to, but even if you only have a shared secretary, and various people around you whose job descriptions are similar to your own, there are probably a lot of tasks you can pass on.

Tell Us Your Stories

Are you lazy sometimes? A lot of the time? All of the time? We'd like to hear about how it's worked for you. Write to us. Give us the gory details. We're so lazy, we might just put it in our next book.

U.S. Mail:	Rich and Brian
	P.O. Box 268
	Easton, PA 18042
E-mail:	LAYLOW@FAST.NET